Asking the
Right
Questions

Asking the
Right
Questions

Tools and Techniques for Teamwork

Edie L. Holcomb

CORWIN PRESS, INC.
A Sage Publications Company
Thousand Oaks, California

For information address:

Corwin Press, Inc.
A Sage Publications Company
2455 Teller Road
Thousand Oaks, California 91320
email: order@corwin.sagepub.com

SAGE Publications Ltd.
6 Bonhill Street
London EC2A 4PU
United Kingdom

SAGE Publications India Pvt. Ltd.
M-32 Market
Greater Kailash I
New Delhi 110 048 India

Printed in the United States of America

Library of Congress Cataloging-in-Publication Data

Holcomb, Edie L.
    Asking the right questions : tools and techniques for teamwork /
Edie L. Holcomb.
      p. cm.
    Includes bibliographical references (pp. 120-123) and index.
    ISBN 0-8039-6357-2 (alk. paper) — ISBN 0-8039-6358-0 (pbk. :
alk. paper)
      1. Group work in education—United States. 2. Team learning
approach in education—United States. 3. Educational change—United
States. 4. School management and organization—United States.
I. Title.
LB1032.H64   1996
371.3'95—dc20   95-43337

This book is printed on acid-free paper.

96 97 98 99 00 10 9 8 7 6 5 4 3 2 1

Corwin Press Production Editor: S. Marlene Head

Contents

Foreword   vii
by Shirley M. Hord

Acknowledgments   x

About the Author   xii

1. Introduction   1

   • Scenario 1 • Scenario 2 • Scenario 3 • Synthesis

2. Asking the Right Questions   8

   • Scenario 2, Act 2 • Refinement of the Five Critical
   Questions • The Five Questions and Three Models of
   Change • Overview

3. Answering the "Where Are We Now?" Question   14

   • Histograms • Pie Charts • Run Charts • Surveys
   • Focus Groups • Pareto Charts • Think, Pair, Share
   • Flowcharting

4. Answering the "Where Do We Want to Go?" Question   40

   • Affinity Process • Brainstorming • Nominal Group
   Process • Color Coding • Weighted Voting

5. Answering the "How Will We Get There?" Question   59

    • Cause-and-Effect Diagram (Fishbone) • Force Field Analysis • Decision Matrix • Action Planning

6. Answering the "How Will We Know We Are (Getting) There?" Question   78

    • Are We Reaching Our Goals? • Are We Coping With Change? • Are We Fulfilling Our Mission?

7. Answering the "How Will We Sustain the Focus and Momentum?" Question   86

    • Continue Training and Coaching • Cope With Conflict • Engage in Sustained Inquiry • Refocus and Reaffirm Organizational Values • Support Leaders and Followers

8. Bonus Questions   112

    • Did It Make Sense Then? Does It Make Sense Now? • Who Else . . . Should Be Included? • Who Else . . . if Not Me?

9. Using the Matrix   116

    • As a Quick Index to Your Toolbox • As a Tool for Planning Personal Skill Development • As a Tool for Designing Team Training • As a Tool for Coaching New Facilitators • Conclusion

Annotated Bibliography   120

Index   124

Foreword

If you don't have a hammer,
a shoe will do.

That myth is dispelled in this book that offers assistance to school-based teams and their leaders as they guide and support schools in their change and improvement efforts. Most everyone agrees that schools should be about the business of increasing their effectiveness, and many volumes have been written to advance this goal. None, however, has provided the leaders and facilitators of the school improvement process with the kind of down-to-earth information and guidance for conducting the day-to-day work of school change and improvement that this book does.

Asking the Right Questions: Tools and Techniques for Teamwork is both elegantly written and eminently easy to read. Its practical content entices the school leader along, to learn what this volume has to offer: both wit and wisdom about a finely honed compendium of tools and techniques, along with tips and strategies for when and how to use them.

The book is organized thoughtfully around five questions that represent phases or stages of the school improvement process:

- Where are we now?
- Where do we want to go?
- How will we get there?
- How will we know we are (getting) there?
- How will we sustain the focus and momentum?

Tools that are most relevant to each of the phases are identified. A consistent outline identifies each tool's purpose, when to use it, who to involve, and materials that are needed. It also provides tips for facilitators and an example of each tool's application. This arrangement and description of the tools makes for user-friendly accessibility of the information by school improvement leaders and facilitators. A sample of the tools includes histograms, surveys, run charts, weighted voting, force field analysis, decision matrices, and many others. Some of these tools will be familiar to school leadership teams, but their applications may be new. Others will be unfamiliar but available for new learning.

No one is better able to provide school leaders with tools that add rigor and precision to their daily operations than Edie Holcomb. She has been a campus leader of school reform and has experienced and studied the process at the personal and practical learning levels. She has trained and developed others, preparing them for the role of leaders of change. To do this, she has developed training materials and activities and has served as a national and international presenter and disseminator of the materials.

In the text, her stories of practice at the campus and district levels come from personal experiences that encompass a wide range of roles and responsibilities. Her use of colorful metaphors contributes richly to the descriptions and explanations of the requirements of the school change journey—a trip she has made many times. Her own hands-on experiences are reflected in the information she shares, for example, in her reference to the "TYNT-NYNT syndrome, this-year's-new-thing soon replaced by next-year's-new-thing" (p. 7).

In short, Edie Holcomb has been in the trenches as a school practitioner learning about change. But she also has taken the opportunity as a school change trainer to analyze and study the process from the developer's perspective. In addition, she has been a student of the research literature, enhancing her knowledge base while serving on faculty in higher education. These various plateaus and perspectives of the world have contributed to her thoughtful observations and advice such as "Only through sensitivity to the past can change agents link innovation with events remembered fondly and disassociate new practices from those that have bitter legacies" (p. 14). She tells it like an insider—and an outsider—as one who has been in both places.

With this broad background, Holcomb makes a rich contribution to the resources for school change leaders and facilitators. Everyone who holds responsibility for guiding and supporting schools in their reform and improvement endeavors will find much of value in this book.

Shirley M. Hord
Southwest Educational Development Laboratory
Austin, Texas

Acknowledgments

This book is dedicated to the memory of my minister-father, Warren E. Holcomb, who continued to nurture me through adulthood, providing daily demonstrations of lifelong learning and servant leadership.

It could not have been written without the opportunities, assistance, and support provided by many individuals and groups. I offer my apologies to those I will inevitably omit and extend grateful thanks to:

Lee F. Olsen, my husband, who encouraged me to submit my outline, prompted me to get started, and—when it seemed impossible to finish—knew me so well that by telling me it was okay to quit gave me the very motivation I needed to finish.

Richard Rossmiller, professor emeritus, University of Wisconsin, who was my boss, colleague, role model, and coauthor and became a lifetime friend by introducing me to my husband.

Barb Furlong, true friend, who first suggested I develop a chart and then told me there was "at least an article" in it.

Dennis Glaeser, napkin-doodling colleague from Wisconsin's CESA 6, for his draft of the five critical questions.

Dave Pedersen and Jody Bublitz, technical assistants, for turning my scribbles into a matrix and my wall charts into figures.

Barbara O. Taylor, cofounder of the National Center for Effective Schools, for exemplifying perseverance in pursuit of her vision.

My colleagues in Poudre School District for sharing a work environment that enabled me to revive this project.

Dedicated educators in Arizona, Arkansas, Colorado, Florida, Indiana, Iowa, Kentucky, Louisiana, Michigan, New Jersey, New York, Ohio, Oregon, South Carolina, Texas, Virginia, Wisconsin, Guam, Canada, St. Lucia, and Hong Kong, whose work to improve their schools provides examples for this book and for the professional lives of all of us.

About the Author

Edie L. Holcomb is highly regarded for her ability to link research and practice on issues related to school leadership, improvement, and reform. She holds a B.S. in elementary education, an M.S. in gifted education, and an Ed.S. in educational administration. She received her Ph.D. in educational administration from the University of Minnesota. Her background includes teaching experience at all grade levels and administrative experience at the building and district level in Illinois, Alabama, Minnesota, South Dakota, Iowa, and Wisconsin. She served as Associate Director of the National Center for Effective Schools, developing *School-Based Instructional Leadership*, a training program for site-based teams. She has provided technical assistance for implementation of school improvement efforts throughout the United States and in Canada, Guam, St. Lucia, and Hong Kong. Her recent work has included synthesizing change efforts such as outcome-based education and total quality management with existing school improvement frameworks. As Associate Professor of Educational Administration at Wichita State University in Kansas, Edie coordinated the principalship course and internships and taught applied inquiry in the field-based doctoral program. She now serves as Organizational Development Specialist for the Poudre School District in Fort Collins, Colorado, which includes consulting with principals and teams on their school improvement processes.

1

Introduction

Scenario 1

Why does the phone ring only when something's on the stove, my hands are in the sink, my body's in the bathtub, or my mind is in some other state? This time when it jangled, my wet body was in Wisconsin while my mind was in Michigan grappling with the needs of my recently widowed mom and trying to fast-forward myself through the stages of grief. An unfamiliar voice on the other end asked, "Is this the Edie Holcomb who's been consulting with the Restructuring Committee?" As I acknowledged that identity, mental red lights and alarm bells kicked in full force. Reporter? Board member? Misinformed nonparticipant? "Well, my name is John Doe.[1] I'm on the scheduling committee at our high school and we've been studying a four-period day, and that's what we want to recommend to the whole faculty. But there's going to be a lot of resistance and I was told you know a lot of group processes and I'm wondering if you could recommend the approach that would work best." The relief that it wasn't the media was followed by sheer panic as my mental screen went absolutely blank, and I asked myself: "If I'm the Edie Holcomb who knows a lot of group process techniques, why can't I think of a single one right now? I need a 'crib sheet' to hang by every phone in this house so I can remember what I know when I get these 'cold calls'"!

Scenario 2

A few days later, body clothed but mind in a state of frustration, I looked around a large square of tables at a room full of staff developers from intermediate and state education agencies. I had been hired by this group for three purposes: to present the effective schools research as a knowledge base, then introduce and apply findings on school change processes, and finally integrate components of the state's approach to Goals 2000 and other state standards. These outcomes were to be achieved in three once-a-month workshops. Only one had occurred so far.

The planning session had deteriorated into a defense of each agency's preferred model for school change as most current, most comprehensive, and most worthy of becoming a statewide model. Sincere, conscientious professionals who had spent the coffee break bemoaning the difficulties of breaking down departmental barriers in high schools were engaged in their own turf wars, talking at cross-purposes about the same concepts, each armed with his or her particular guru's customized vocabulary. This time I asked myself, "Why is this happening, even in a group that knows better? What we need is a set of factors that are common to all these processes, use no educational jargon, and have no capital letters to turn into acronyms!"

Scenario 3

Coffee cups and cookie crumbs littered the table as the apprehensive group of principals wrestled with the role changes occurring as a result of the district's mandate for site-based management. Official job descriptions and evaluation systems remained unchanged, but every building was to form a school council, and the administrators would be held responsible for its success. Even those most optimistic, cheering up the others with the potential for greater autonomy and authentic shared decision making, wondered whether they had the knowledge and skills to pull it off. One voice rose above the rest. "I'm supposed to form a team and I don't even know who should be on it or what it should do. No one in my school—not even me—has ever been to a workshop on teamwork. We need some training first, but we have to start without it. What we need is an outline of the things we'll need to know and which ones come first, so we can learn as we go."

Synthesis

Some wise—or at least widely quoted—person said that important things come in threes. True or not, the aphorism applies because these three episodes happened within the space of a few weeks and resulted in the matrix around which this book has developed (see Figure 1.1).

The row of group process techniques across the top is a sideways version of the list I developed as my own skill catalog from which to select, modify, and/or combine tried-and-true methods when presented with a new consulting question or facilitating challenge. Development of the five questions in the left-hand column began in Scenario 2 and is described in more detail in chapter 2. Each of chapters 3-7 provides directions for use of group processes and describes their application in examples from real school experiences. The tips for facilitators and examples are not pure in a research sense and may not satisfy some specialists. There are other group processes that work very well, and there are additional ways to use those included here. I am simply sharing the techniques I know, as I know them, and the settings in which I have been able to help others apply them successfully. Uses of the matrix to assist others like the struggling principals of Scenario 3 are outlined in chapter 9.

This book does not pretend to contribute a vast depository of new knowledge to the field of organizational development and school change. That knowledge is already available, and some helpful sources are listed in the annotated bibliography. What this book adds is practical tips and stories of application and implementation from educational settings. If *Asking the Right Questions: Tools and Techniques for Teamwork* finds a unique niche, it will be as a synthesizer of skills often learned in isolated fragments and of processes that now compete for the "one best way" award. It is neither a scholarly tome on change research nor an exhaustive compendium of detailed exercises defended with psychological rationale. The annotated bibliography is provided to assist the reader with those needs. This is simply a

Where Are We Now? (readiness, planning, and training,[a] initiation[b])	Think, Pair, Share	Flowcharting	Pareto Charts	Pie Charts	Histograms	Run Charts	Surveys	Focus Groups	Affinity Process	Brainstorming	Nominal Group Process	Color Coding	Weighted Voting	Fishbone (Cause and Effect)	Force Field Analysis	Decision Matrix	Action Planning	CBAM-SoCQ	Quick Write	Venn Diagram	Go for the Green	TalkWalk	Action Research	Reflective Study Groups	Active Listening	Networking
Raise awareness of need for change	3	X						X	X	X		X		X					X	X		X		X	X	
Clarify roles and responsibilities	X	X						X	X	X		X							X	X	X	X			X	X
Diagnose motivation for change (source, intensity)	X						X	X										X	X	X					X	
Review existing philosophy, mission, belief statements	X						X	X	X	X		X	X	X					X	X				X	X	
Diagnose governance and program factors	X	3	3				X	X	X			X		X				X	X	X			X	X		
Diagnose student success			X	3	3	3	X	X	X				X		X								X		X	
Diagnose stakeholder perceptions				X	X	X	3	X	X			X	X	X					X	X			X	X	X	
Diagnose organizational culture, climate	X		X				X			X		X		X				X	X	X	X		X		X	X

Figure 1.1. Matrix of Tools for Asking the Right Questions

	1	2	3	4	5	6	7	8	9	10	11	12	13	14	15	16	17
Where Do We Want to Go? (planning and training;[a] initiation;[b] plan[c])																	
Develop/affirm mission statement	X					X	X	4	X		X				X	X	X
Stimulate visioning	X					X	X	4			X				X	X	X
Prioritize concerns		X	X			X	4	4	4		X				X	X	
Set goals/targets with focus on students	X					X	X	4	4						X	X	
Identify best practices								X	X						X	X	
How Will We Get There? (planning, training, and implementation;[a] implementation;[b] plan[c])																	
Identify factors related to concerns	X					X	X	X	X	X	5	X		X	X	X	X
Identify barriers	X	X	X			X	X	X			5			X	X	X	X
Select strategies		X	X			X	X	X	X	5				X		X	
Develop action plans	X								5					X		X	X
Identify indicators/data to monitor	X			X	X	X			X					X		X	X
Affirm mission and beliefs	X					X	X	X	X		X			X		X	X
How Will We Know We Are (Getting) There? (implementation and maintenance;[a] implementation;[b] do and check[c])																	
Monitor progress on identified indicators/data		X	X	X	X	X			X								
Affirm mission and beliefs	X					X	X	X	X		X			X		X	X
Identify and respond to individuals' concerns	X					X	X	X	X	X	X		6	X	X	X	X	X

(continued)

How Will We Sustain the Focus and Momentum? (maintenance,[a] institutionalization,[b] check, act, and plan[c])

Topic	Think, Pair, Share	Flowcharting	Pareto Charts	Pie Charts	Histograms	Run Charts	Surveys	Focus Groups	Affinity Process	Brainstorming	Nominal Group Process	Color Coding	Weighted Voting	Fishbone (Cause and Effect)	Force Field Analysis	Decision Matrix	Action Planning	CBAM-SoCQ	Quick Write	Venn Diagram	Go for the Green	TalkWalk	Action Research	Reflective Study Groups	Active Listening	Networking
Cope with conflict																			7	7	7	7			X	X
Build culture of inquiry																							7	X	X	X
Monitor progress and adjust strategies			X	X	X	X	X	X					X	X	X	X	X				X				X	X
Affirm mission and beliefs	X							X	X	X		X	X					X	X					7	X	X
Support leaders and followers	X							X	X	X		X	X					X			X	X		X	7	7

Note: Numbers in cells indicate the chapter in which the topic is covered.

a. From the RPTIM model (readiness, planning, training, implementation, and maintenance).

b. From the *Three Is* model (initiation, implementation, and institutionalization).

c. From the PDCA cycle (plan-do-check-act).

Figure 1.1. Continued

"what can I do with my group on Monday with the skills I already have" guide for leaders of school-based teams, whether laypersons or experienced educators.

Note

1. Identities of schools and individuals in this book have been slightly altered to respect their privacy.

2

Asking the Right Questions

Scenario 2, Act 2

The tension continued into lunch time. The moderator of the meeting, an administrator with outstanding facilitation skills but limited history with the group, expressed a sense of failure with the lack of progress and a desire to go back to his office where he could accomplish something. The author, who by this time doubted *anyone's* ability to meet the varied expectations of the group, offered to withdraw and let the group clarify what it really wanted and determine whether another presenter would be more suitable for the two remaining sessions. One agency's representative actually gathered her materials and went home. But one dedicated member of the group sat thoughtfully, apparently doodling on his napkin.

When the group reconvened, the reflective participant volunteered his napkin notes, five questions that reflected the themes evolving during the discussion of change models. The questions were as follows:

- Where are we now?
- Where do we want to go?
- How will we get there?
- How will we know we are there?
- How can we keep it going?

This set of questions broke the gridlock, and the remaining participants began to link their desired topics to the five headings. As the content agenda developed, the original direction to ground the workshops in the knowledge base of effective schools research was restated. A focus on findings from school settings was considered essential to counter some educators' resistance to ideas "transplanted" or "borrowed" from business and industry.

Refinement of the Five Critical Questions

The questions generated that day reminded me of the question-answer format used by Larry Lezotte and Barbara Jacoby in their *Guide to the School Improvement Process Based on Effective Schools Research.*

Lezotte and Jacoby describe the school improvement process in five stages: preparation, focus, diagnosis, plan development, and implementation/monitoring. Their guiding question for the focus stage is "Where do we want to go?" Diagnosis includes interpretation of student outcomes and organizational dimensions in response to the question "How are we doing?" Plan development results from consideration of "How will we get to where we want to go?" And the stage of implementation, monitoring, evaluation, and renewal is prompted by the query "How will we know we got there?"

The form of the questions used in this book was also influenced by the work of Michael Fullan and others who have written about realistic expectations for the pace of change in organizations. Writers on school change speak of 3-5 years for a moderately complex change or 5-7 years for major restructuring to move from being an innovation to becoming a routine part of how the organization conducts its primary functions. With those time frames in mind, asking "How will we know we are there?" seemed inadequate. It would imply that monitoring is exclusively summative, occurring at some distant point in the future. Because members of our society are not well known for delayed gratification, motivating continued efforts through proof of successful results would be difficult with a 7-year lag time. The question "How will we know we are there?" became "How will we know we are (getting) there?" The "getting" implies the need for milestones or benchmarks that will verify gradual progress and improvement.

Literature on stages of change also influenced the last question, which here reads "How will we sustain the focus and momentum?" One of the most common problems faced by change agents in schools is the TYNT-NYNT syndrome: "this year's new thing" soon replaced by "next year's new thing." Fullan, Miles, Huberman, and others point out the need to continue a change process from initiation to implementation and on to institutionalization. The "bandwagon" approach so common to school change efforts prevents this sustained momentum. At the same time, Elmore and others have documented that restructuring schools does not merit the time and effort unless it directly affects the aspects of teaching that improve student learning. The importance of maintaining the focus on student outcomes, as well as the momentum of energy and resources, is reflected in the wording of the fifth question.

The Five Questions and Three Models of Change

The five critical questions were then used as the five major sections of the matrix (Fig. 1.1) for matching group process skills with aspects of school improvement efforts. These five sections are also headed by terminology from three well-known models, processes, or descriptions of change. The first is Wood's RPTIM model, a classic from staff development literature. The acronym stands for stages of readiness, planning, training, implementation, and maintenance. The **readiness** stage includes identifying major problems of the school or district, working in collaboration with key groups to develop goals, and examining current practices. The **planning** stage includes identifying differences between goals, desired practices, and actual practices and planning training activities based on that diagnosis. During the **training** stage, all affected groups including central office administrators, principals, teachers, and others receive training and develop, share, and critique action plans. **Implementation** requires that resources are allocated to support new practices and that additional coaching and training are provided on an ongoing basis. The **maintenance** stage involves supervision and monitoring to continue new behaviors and use of feedback to guide further improvement. Although Wood's work focused specifically on staff development and instructional changes, his framework was generalized by school districts and regional labs to guide many effective schools programs.

A second well-known description of change is presented in writings by Miles, Huberman, and Fullan and is often referred to as the

Three Is: initiation, implementation, and institutionalization. A key factor in the **initiation** of change is identification of a high-profile need that participants feel is relevant to them, for which a sense of readiness has been created, and for which resources have been allocated to demonstrate the organization's commitment. The visibility of a few strong advocates who can present a clear model of implementation and actively move it forward are essential aspects of successful initiation.

The **implementation** stage requires attention to unique local characteristics of the community, district, and its principals and teachers. Overall coordination is needed but must be balanced by shared control, which we refer to here as involvement of stakeholders. The balancing of pressure, through conveying clear expectations of progress and improvement while providing support through ongoing technical assistance and rewards, is critical. Fullan's description of essentials for implementation include vision building, initiative taking, staff training, monitoring, and evolutionary planning—with continual adjustment as data and feedback are received and analyzed.

Many change processes survive through initiation, and attempts are made to implement them, but they do not take root and do not become embedded in the culture. Among the reasons this **institutionalization** does not occur are lack of close links to the teaching and learning process and lack of continued training and support until new practices are in widespread use. Continued assistance in the new practice must be accompanied by removal of competing priorities.

Recently, other descriptions of organizational change and improvement have emerged from the total quality management literature. A model that has been applied in schools is the plan-do-check-act (PDCA) cycle. The **plan** stage involves identifying a needed change, assembling available data and collecting new data to clarify what needs to occur, and identifying root causes of the problem. To **do** means to generate possible solutions, select and implement them on a pilot basis, and gather data on the results. A **check** verifies what has been accomplished, what worked well and what did not, and analyzes results before implementing an attempted solution on a broader scale. Decisions are made to **act** on the results by abandoning the new practice or standardizing it to ensure consistency throughout the organization. Processes are continually monitored, and the cycle is repeated.

Overview

Chapter 3 describes group processes that can be used to explore the question "Where are we now?" These steps include aspects of the readiness, planning, and training stages of RPTIM and are comparable to the initiation stage. One indicator of an organization's readiness to change is its willingness to take a hard look at itself. This involves the formation of leadership groups that will coordinate data collection and interpretation in the vital areas of student performance, stakeholder perceptions, and organizational culture.

In this book, the term *stakeholders* is used to refer to all who have a stake in the use of resources and in the skills and knowledge that students will possess when they leave the system. Parents are usually the first group mentioned in a listing of stakeholders, but they represent a declining segment of the taxpayers who support the schools. The term *community* is used here in a broader way to include social service agencies, businesses, and taxpayers who do not have children attending school. There are also internal stakeholders, for every employee of the district—administrator, teacher, social and health worker, clerical, custodial, food and transportation provider—is affected by how the organization functions. The interactions between and among these groups establish the culture of the organization, which should also be diagnosed in answer to the "Where are we now?" question.

Chapter 4 provides activities that challenge a school or district to reach consensus about "Where do we want to go?" This question compares with the RPTIM stages of planning and training, additional work on initiation, and the plan tasks of PDCA. At this stage, mission statements are written, clarified with sets of belief statements, or revived and made a part of daily practice and decision making. Priority concerns must be established, and factors that contribute to those problem areas identified. Subquestions dealt with through the activities described in chapter 4 include "What should it really look like?" and "Why isn't it that way now?"

A strategic action plan will result from answering the "How will we get there?" question. Attention must be given to the critical elements of planning, training, and implementation, as described in all three models of change. Unfortunately, too many schools leap into planning without devoting adequate time to study best practices that address their priority concerns, make comparisons with their current practices, and select the strategies that have been proven effective in achieving their desired results. Materials and tips to use in these preliminary planning stages are presented in chapter 5.

Answering the question "How will we know we are (getting) there?" generates even more need to collect data and inject life into the school's mission statement. It parallels the work of implementation and maintenance, and it begins the do and check phases of PDCA. Chapter 6 describes a visioning process that results in observable indicators that can be monitored. Visible results of the actions taken provide both the "carrot" and the "stick" to sustain the difficult effort of school change. Success breeds success, and evidence of progress motivates sustained effort. Regular monitoring of key indicators conveys a strong message that change is an expectation.

The most complex question of all seems to be "How will we sustain the focus and momentum?" Attention must be given to all the critical elements of maintenance, institutionalization, and the PDCA tasks of do, check, and act. The need for monitoring continues, but a shift must occur to make the need and motivation for change more internal. Techniques such as reflective study groups and action research engage participants through their own interest areas. True courage is needed to identify nonproductive practices and abandon them. At the same time, relationships between and among groups and participants must be maintained and strengthened through problem solving and conflict resolution. Activities and processes to achieve these ends are presented in chapter 7.

Chapter 8 presents bonus questions that can be used to ameliorate the anxiety and loss of efficacy often experienced during change. Chapter 9 concludes with discussions for personalization of the matrix and a variety of uses for professional growth and consultation.

3

Answering the
"Where Are We Now?"
Question

There are travelers, and then there are ramblers. Travelers follow their maps, and ramblers follow their noses. Travelers have a destination in mind, and they lay out a route from here to there. Knowing the starting point is just as important as knowing the destination if the journey is to be safe, accurate, timely, and cost effective. Travelers also check weather conditions, make lists, and assemble needed items. In short, ramblers say "Let's go somewhere." Travelers say, "Let's gather some information, make a plan, and *then* go."

The journey of school change is never an easy one, and there are many hazards along the way, but the trip can get off to its smoothest start by carefully analyzing the present situation. This chapter includes tips and techniques for addressing the question "Where are we now?" At least three critical aspects of the school's or district's status must be included: student performance, stakeholder perceptions, and organizational culture.

When we think of data on student performance, our instinctive response is to visualize graphs of test scores and leave it at that. This initial limited scope implies that acquisition of discrete bits of knowledge is the sole and complete function of the school and gives the test makers more credit than they deserve. If a school or district justifies its test results with claims that "these tests don't cover all the things we try to accomplish in school," that organization must identify ways to demonstrate that it does accomplish all those other things. Desirable student results like citizenship are more clearly revealed in data such as attendance, participation in service activities, and occurrences of vandalism and disruptive behavior.

Schools and districts must acknowledge the reality that public education is a service industry that must be user friendly or lose its "market share" to vouchers, private schools, and for-profit enterprises. Surveys, telephone interviews, and focus groups are among the methods often used to gather stakeholder perceptions. Gathering the information, however, is only the first step and can do more harm than good if not followed by analyzing, interpreting, and reporting the results back to the constituents and using them in goal setting and planning for improvement.

The school culture includes roles and relationships, the history of and motivation for prior change in the organization, and an awareness of governance and program factors that may inhibit or enhance new efforts. Only through sensitivity to the past can change agents link innovation with events remembered fondly and disassociate new practices from those that have left bitter legacies.

This chapter describes group processes that can be employed to help a school or district ask itself, "Where are we now?" Each description includes the purpose of the group technique, appropriate timing, recommended participants, materials needed, and tips to guide the facilitator.

Histograms

Every school improvement effort I have encountered has espoused "increased student achievement" as its foundation. Given that commonality, I have been amazed at the number of school improvement plans that include no references to student performance or goals that relate to the process of teaching and learning. In fact, when most districts report on student performance, they use a mean (average) score based on aggregate (all scores mixed together) data. This type of reporting has contributed to myths like the "Lake Wobegon effect" that "all the children are above average." Schools and districts with homogeneous populations and a strong, cultural work ethic are lulled into complacency by mean scores that rank favorably with schools and districts facing far greater challenges. Use of a histogram to depict student performance can provide more accurate information and a better analysis of the current performance level of students and the school's success at teaching.

Purpose. A histogram is a type of bar chart that shows a distribution of information. It allows educators to see the range and variation in student achievement, rather than an overall average score. This provides a much better picture of how well the school is fulfilling its obligation to teach all children.

When to use. An examination of current student performance should be one of the early steps in addressing the "Where are we now?" question. The same analysis should be conducted each time a general assessment is used, and each set of results should be added to the longitudinal trend data being accumulated.

Whom to involve. School psychologists and counselors are valuable members of a work group that is compiling data on student achievement and behavior. The group should also include teachers who work with the student population in the subject areas (of a cognitive assessment) or in the school environment (in case of behavior). Although test data may initially be compiled by specialists like the testing companies, or school district research and evaluation departments, interpretation of what the data mean should be done in concert with the teachers who work with the students on a daily basis. It is difficult to engage teachers in the use of data, especially if they are demeaned by having data returned to them with weak areas or low scores already highlighted as if they can't make those distinctions themselves.

Materials needed. A histogram can be constructed to represent any type of data available and relevant for discussion, for example, test scores, grades, attendance, and discipline referrals. A laptop computer and appropriate software can make the job easier, but there is learning value in having groups do a rough draft of their histogram on paper.

TIPS FOR FACILITATORS

The first step is to create a frequency distribution of scores, number of absences, or other factor. The second step is to divide the full range of scores into a usable number of categories or classes. In the case of achievement scores, testing companies often array the scores in stanines. Another good set of categories for examining student performance is the use of quartiles. This divides scores into those that fall between the 1st to 25th percentiles, 26th to 50th percentiles, 51st to 75th, and 76th percentile and above. A histogram with one high bar in the third quartile may verify that a commendable mean of 70th percentile really represents success of all students. If the histogram has a high bar in the third or fourth quartile, but also in the lowest quartile, it can indicate that there are enough high-achieving students to influence the mean and mask the reality that the school is not meeting its obligation to another segment of its population.

FOR EXAMPLE

Figure 3.1 is actually a combination of eight histograms. The math scores for each grade level are represented in quartiles. It only takes a glance to discover that the distribution of performance provides a lot more information than a mean score for the entire grade. Graphic displays like the histogram provide some answers. They are just as valuable in prompting more questions. Groups should be challenged to discuss the following questions: What else might this tell us? What do we do with this information? and What do we want these histograms to look like 3 years from now? The last question is particularly important if a school has not used data in the past and only has the "snapshot" data of the current year to use as a baseline.

A VARIATION

The histogram is introduced in this chapter as one example of how graphs can display data in ways that are understandable and that prompt further examination of student learning. Many schools with heterogeneous populations have made commitments to equity and want to know whether the distribution of performance is the same for all groups within the total student population. Factors such as race/ethnicity and socioeconomic status (SES) are often considered. In Figure 3.2, the performance scores have been separated to compare the distribution of scores for students from low-SES homes with those from more affluent settings.

The process of breaking up data to examine the performance of different subgroups is called disaggregation. Although this histogram shows that 63% of all students rank in the top two quartiles, it also points out that only 37% and 39% of the students from minority groups achieve at this level.

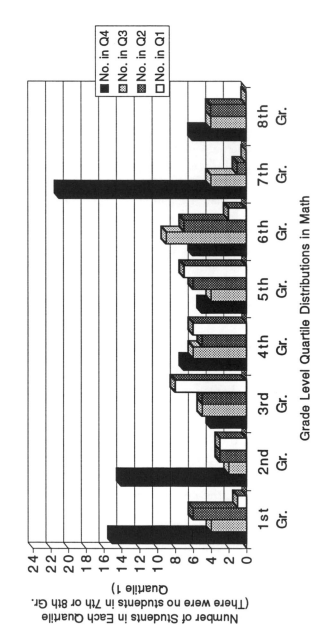

Figure 3.1. Histogram of Student Achievement

18

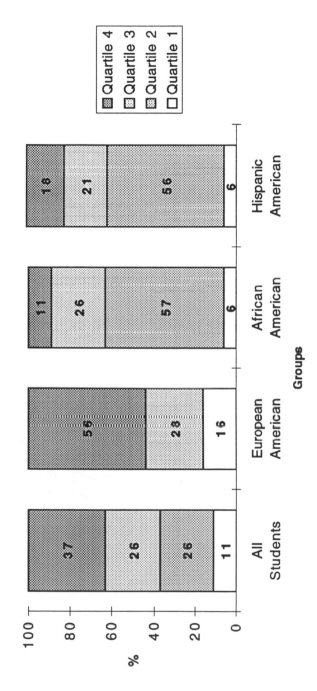

Figure 3.2. Histogram of Disaggregated Student Achievement

19

ANOTHER TWIST

The term *student performance* can encompass more than academic success. Schools often have other expectations that relate to goals such as good citizenship. These schools may use data such as attendance, punctuality, completion of assignments, participation in service projects, behavior, and vandalism to assess how well the school is helping students develop characteristics of good citizenship. Such data can also be displayed in histograms to help a school ask itself, "Where are we now in terms of student performance?"

Pie Charts

A pie chart is another way to display data that is easy to understand and interpret. Like the histogram, it can help to answer the "Where are we now?" question by describing the current situation.

Purpose. The pie chart is particularly useful for demonstrating how a resource is used. Time, money, materials, and personnel are resources that must be used efficiently to help schools be as effective as possible in serving students and their communities.

When to use. Pie charts can be useful when you need to describe how a resource is divided for various uses. It can also show how students are divided into various groups, courses, or activities.

Whom to involve. The important aspect of involvement with any use of data is that those who are part of the situation being analyzed are included in both gathering the information initially and then analyzing and interpreting it. When people are directly involved in collecting the data, they are much more likely to accept the results as an accurate representation of their situation.

Materials needed. Developing the pie chart can easily be done by any individual using paper and pencil or software graphics.

TIPS FOR FACILITATORS

Pie charts work best when there are a limited number of slices in the pie. If a resource is divided into so many different uses that the pie would have many slivers, it will not be as effective in delivering the

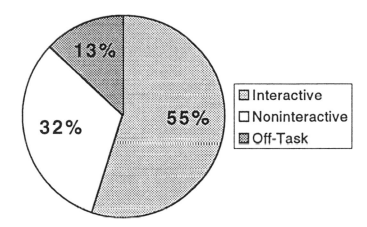

Figure 3.3. Pie Chart of Student Instructional Time Audit

information at a glance, and another type of graph or table should be used.

FOR EXAMPLE

The pie chart in Figure 3.3 illustrates the use of a very important resource—instructional time. Students were observed in classrooms, and their behavior was tallied as interactive, noninteractive, and off-task. With very few words of explanation, it is easy to see that students were actively engaged over half the time.

Run Charts

The histogram, pie chart, and most other graphs represent information at a certain point in time. In contrast, the run chart can illustrate trends in data over a span of time.

Purpose. The purpose of the run chart is to monitor a situation or process over time to identify changes. Although the histograms in Figure 3.1 show distribution of student achievement on one year's scores, a run chart would show how those same students score from one year to the next, and whether their achievement improves, declines, or stays the same.

When to use. If a school or district has been collecting data over a period of time, a run chart can be constructed in the early stages of addressing the "Where are we now?" question. Sometimes schools have not used test scores or other data in any systematic way, and they can go back and re-create a run chart to show a history of what has been occurring. In other cases, schools can only gather data for the first time now and use the data as a baseline. As the same data are analyzed every year, a run chart is gradually developed.

Whom to involve. As with all work using data, those who partici- pate in the process under study must be involved in collection and analysis.

Materials needed. Construction of the run chart itself can be done with pencil and paper or using computer graphics.

TIPS FOR FACILITATORS

The left-hand, vertical side of the run chart is called the y-axis and usually shows the criteria or factor being analyzed, such as percent- age of dropouts or number of absences. The horizontal line across the bottom of the run chart is called the x-axis and represents the periods of time being measured, such as class periods, days, or years. Be sure to clearly label both the vertical and horizontal axes.

One problem with a run chart is that observers tend to overreact to any fluctuation in the line. They may give themselves too much credit for any upturn or become overly dismayed by any downturn. A rule of thumb is to look for at least seven data points in a consistent direction before concluding that true change has occurred. It is inter- esting that this recommendation from statisticians corresponds so well with comments by educational change experts, who say that it takes 5 to 7 years to institutionalize new practices.

FOR EXAMPLE

The school that created Figure 3.4 had disaggregated its reading scores and discovered an achievement gap related to SES. The school's improvement plans focused on improvement of reading performance for all students and greater equity in achievement. Fig- ure 3.4 reports the scores each year and shows a consistent direction of improved performance and narrowing of the gap between low-SES and middle-to-upper-SES students.

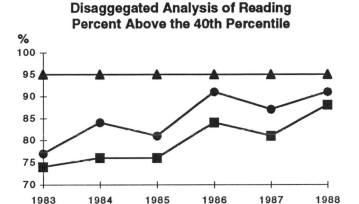

Figure 3.4. Run Chart of Reading Scores

Surveys

The histogram, pie chart, and run chart were introduced to help answer the question "Where are we now?" in terms of student achievement. A school, district, or any other organization also needs to know where it stands with its customers, clients, and community.

Purpose. In the business environment, surveys are used to measure customer satisfaction. In much the same way, school leaders use surveys to learn what stakeholders think about the school. Stakeholders in an educational enterprise include internal groups, such as students, teachers, administrators, and support staff, and external groups, such as parents, taxpayers without students in the home, and businesses that employ the graduates of the system. The annotated bibliography can direct you to formal surveys that have been developed with separate forms for students, staff, and parents that may include services for compiling and analyzing responses for an additional fee. The informal survey that is locally designed to get information on a specific aspect of the school, in a timely manner, is also valuable. Consultation with an expert in survey design greatly increases the usefulness of the instrument and the data it generates.

When to use. Formal surveys, especially those packaged with forms for various stakeholder groups, are most helpful when school leaders have limited experience collecting and using data. They can provide a level of comfort, a fair degree of reliability, and an aura of objectivity that is especially needed when the idea and experience of receiving outside feedback is unfamiliar. These instruments gather a wide range of overall perceptions on factors that research has linked to school effectiveness. This type of major survey should be conducted at the beginning of a school improvement process and replicated only after sufficient intervals to measure change. Many consultants suggest an interval of 3 years. Shorter, informal surveys can be used successfully at any point in a change process to gather recommendations on a specific problem or gauge reaction to a new innovation.

Whom to involve. For many years, schools were encouraged to survey every member of every stakeholder group, and results were regarded as representative because of the widespread distribution of the survey. Unfortunately, many locally developed surveys fail to ask the right questions. And few school leaders have the statistical background to ask crucial questions about the results, such as the rate of return and whether returns came from all parts of the school's attendance area. In one city, a major program decision was made at the district level based on "community input." It was not until implementation of the decision encountered resistance of epic proportions that someone noticed that the rate of return of the surveys was just over 1% of households and that the surveys were almost entirely from one board member's jurisdiction. The use of stratified sampling is now applied more often and is described in Tips for Facilitators.

As with every other type of data analysis, it is important that those who are part of the process being studied are involved in determining how the surveys will be administered and how the results will be analyzed and interpreted.

Materials needed. Surveys have budget implications. The formal surveys from outside sources may be expensive. For locally developed surveys, printing costs may be a factor. Internal staff time must be provided for distribution and collection. If a survey consists primarily of multiple-choice items, bubble sheets and a scanner can shorten analysis time. If surveys are to be mailed to and/or from households, postage costs must also be considered.

Tips for Facilitators

If a school leadership group is developing its own survey, it is important to devote substantial discussion time to "exactly what is it that we want and need to know." Because shorter surveys get better return rates than long ones, it is important to focus the items around the most essential information. Item responses should also be carefully constructed. For example, if response choices are *agree, disagree,* and *don't know,* surveyors will be amazed at the degree of ignorance revealed. Using a reference book on survey construction or including someone with research background on the team is strongly recommended.

A resource person would also provide a more detailed explanation of stratified sampling. In simple language, it means deciding who the major groups are within the total population to be surveyed. Within that group, a certain percentage would be chosen at random. Survey forms may be coded by number or printed on different-colored sheets of paper. When they are returned, a tally can be kept of how many returns there are from each constituency. This will influence how the responses are interpreted and used.

For Example

A school in a very heterogeneous area of the city wanted to gather parents' perceptions about the school and their role in it. The team had been using information from an earlier survey that indicated a high percentage of favorable responses such as "I feel welcome at my school," "I know how to get answers to my questions," and so forth. Based on their data, team members were puzzled by a recent letter to the editor accusing the school of being unfriendly to minority families, and they decided to repeat their survey. This time, they consulted with a parent who was also a realtor, and they determined how various neighborhoods within their attendance area were classified. Using the address field in their student database, they identified 10% of the families in each area and color coded the response sheets. Lots of pink ones came back, and the data verified their earlier survey. But almost no green or blue forms were returned. After several discussions, one member of the group initiated the idea of having the survey introduced by someone familiar to those parents, on their own territory.

In one case, the association president of a subsidized housing project agreed to call people together and explain the survey. A local minister in another area agreed to invite a school representative to meet with a parent group at the church on a weeknight. The surveys were completed and returned, and they verified the letter to the editor. These parents did not feel welcome and did not know how to approach the school. As a result of this extra effort, the tone of discussions about parents who don't care changed radically, and the school began to revise their methods of parent communication and conferencing.

Focus Groups

Many experts on survey construction will recommend at least one open-ended item to allow respondents to create their own answers. The difficulty is that few school leadership groups have the skill and time to do a thematic analysis of all these varied responses. Too often, they make for great lounge reading and speculation on who might have written them but provide little specific direction for planning. Focus groups can meet this need for unstructured responses in a more efficient and useful way.

Purpose. The purpose of a focus group is to build face-to-face communication and get more specific information than a survey might provide. Focus groups may be held to gather perceptions regarding the school's effectiveness on a particular factor, such as parent involvement. They can also be used to clarify survey responses and recommend changes that would be helpful.

When to use. Use a focus group when you need more specific information than a survey could provide, or when a question is so complex that you have not been able to construct a survey item or design response options that seem appropriate. A focus group can also be used as part of the analysis and interpretation of data already gathered.

Whom to involve. A focus group generally includes 10-12 individuals who have personal experience with the question being discussed. If the issue is parent involvement, or if the purpose is to clarify parent responses to a survey or situation, the focus group should be made up of parents. In schools with racial or economic diversity, focus groups should be formed from each population so they can express their views in a comfortable setting with peers. If an issue is student behavior, there may be a focus group of staff and one of parents, but the significant involvement of students themselves should not be overlooked. Ideally, parents, teachers, and students would discuss issues together, and some schools reach this point. Most schools need time to build bridges of trust and respect before a mixed group can be as candid as a focus group should be.

Materials needed. Inviting the right people to a focus group requires knowledge of who the opinion leaders are and skill in building rapport. Other materials needed are a comfortable setting and a tape recorder or process observer with a laptop computer.

TIPS FOR FACILITATORS

When contacting people to serve on a focus group, be clear about what you will be discussing, about the composition of the group, and that you will be recording their comments for future reference, but in a way that is anonymous and confidential.

Assemble the group in a circle of comfortable chairs or around a table where the participants can face each other. The facilitator should not be seated in a place that implies leadership or authority. Refreshments and an opportunity for introductions and get-acquainted chatter are important.

If a tape recorder is being used, people must know of its use, but it should be placed in an unobtrusive location. If a process observer is taking notes on a laptop computer, that person should sit outside the circle. The advantage of using a computer is that it saves the time and extra step of transcribing from a tape. Keyboards have become much quieter, and the noise is usually lost in the sounds of the discussion after just a few minutes.

The facilitator should have a few key questions prepared but should not be tied to them. An opening statement should be made about why this group was formed and what kind of information the school needs. Assure the group that specific examples are needed and will be held in confidence. Let the conversation flow, and resist the temptation to fill any moment of silence with another structured question. As in teaching, "wait time" produces more analytical thinking and more accurate answers.

For Example

The leadership team had administered a formal survey, developed by a highly respected consultant group, based on school effectiveness research. Most of the responses made sense. There were no surprises except for negative parent responses regarding the format of parent-teacher conferences and "student recognition." The task force was cochaired by two members of the school improvement team and included volunteers who agreed to help analyze the survey data. They were not too concerned about the parent conference item. Teachers had talked for some time about how they needed to make different arrangements for these important communication opportunities. But they *were* quite distressed about the "student recognition" item, and they began to list all the ways in which students were recognized for good work, good behavior, helping others, and so forth. They wondered what more they could do and were about to propose a subcommittee to explore ways to get funding from local businesses to provide more student incentives, when one member said, "I wonder what parents thought student recognition means." After a few moments of silent confusion, a first-year teacher timidly suggested, "Maybe we should ask them." It sounded like a pretty logical next move, and the principal helped identify members of a focus group, who were invited to come and discuss the items on the parent survey and what they thought of as they read them. Through the focus group, school leaders discovered that the "student recognition" parents wanted was for the principal to know their children's names, and for all teachers to get to know even the students who were not in their classes and to address them by name—or at least with more respect than "Hey, kid." The face-to-face communication of a focus group shifted the attention of staff from initiating more extrinsic reward systems to looking at the culture of the school and the interactions between staff and students.

Pareto Charts

Surveys and focus groups can identify areas that need improvement. Pareto charts break down aspects of a problem area into more specific causes and help school leaders identify "where to start" to improve the situation.

Purpose. Use a pareto chart when many factors may be involved in a situation, and you need to know which to address first. A pareto chart is a form of vertical bar graph. Its unique feature is that it presents items in order of frequency so a group can deal with "first things first."

When to use. A pareto chart may be helpful after a survey or focus group has been conducted and a wide range of problems has been generated or recommendations proposed. A pareto chart can also display data on aspects of student behavior, such as various factors that cause students to be absent.

Whom to involve. A pareto chart can be constructed by one person. Discussion of what the data mean and what to do about them should involve representatives of those who provided the data (such as survey respondents) and those who have responsibility for the factors described in the data.

Materials needed. A pareto chart can be constructed using the data with paper and pencil or computer software.

TIPS FOR FACILITATORS

Like the run chart, a pareto chart has horizontal and vertical axes that must be clearly labeled. Sometimes data have identified a problem but provide no information on probable causes or related factors. It may be necessary to brainstorm what these causes or factors may be, and gather another set of data. The results are displayed like a bar graph or histogram, but with the factors placed in descending order of frequency.

In most cases, efforts toward improvement should begin with the factors that have the tallest bars. However, common sense must prevail. If even a small percentage of cases are caused by some factor that is dangerous or may have legal ramifications, those situations must be addressed immediately.

FOR EXAMPLE

The staff at one school was concerned about the number of students sent to the office for disciplinary reasons. They wondered whether student behavior was getting worse, whether the offenses

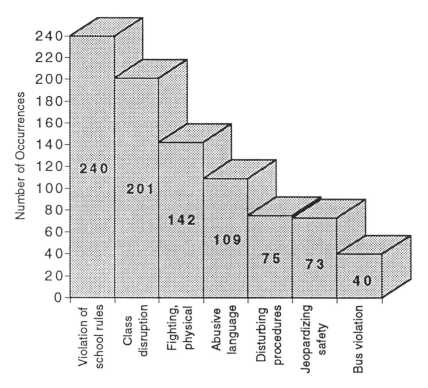

Figure 3.5. Pareto Chart of Student Discipline

actually merited the principal's attention, and what relationship there might be to the new discipline policy that had been developed the summer before. They analyzed the reasons stated on the "pink slips" that students carried with them to the office and constructed the pareto chart in Figure 3.5.

First, they noticed that the greatest number of discipline referrals were related to violating school rules, outlined in their new policy. This discovery led them to reconsider the consequences in the policy and build in more responsibility at the classroom level before sending students out of the room. They also acknowledged that they could have been more conscientious about teaching the new rules to students and communicating them to parents.

The second bar on the pareto chart prompted a decision to provide classroom management training for teachers to help them be more proactive in preventing classroom disruptions in the first place. By the time they got to the third bar, they discovered that the cause they were most worried about (physical violence) was not the most frequent problem, and when they compared it to previous years, fighting had not increased at all.

Note that a total of 880 discipline occurrences were analyzed. Addressing just the first two causes would affect just over half (441) of the incidents analyzed. Without the pareto chart, the school staff might have worked very hard to reduce fighting—certainly a valid effort—but with far less success at reducing the sheer number of students standing in line at the office.

A VARIATION

Teachers from a middle school in a deteriorating section of the city were attending a graduate course on total quality improvement. Their assignment was to work as a quality improvement team on a problem within their school. They had become concerned about the number of transient students who were housed in homeless shelters within their attendance area, and they decided to make that issue a focus of their study. Caring members of the staff had begun trying to find clothing for the students and made other efforts to help them but felt frustrated and overwhelmed. They didn't think the school could function as a social service agency, but they were very aware of the economic neediness of these children.

To gather data for their project, the graduate students decided to conduct private interviews with the homeless students who were now attending the school and find out what they most wanted. They particularly anticipated responses like clothing and social acceptance and feared that they would get data they would not be able to do anything about. When they came to the next class, they were carrying a pareto chart and wearing expressions of amazement and chagrin. The tallest bar on their pareto chart identified a perceived need for security guards. These students had moved away from a major inner-city area where crime was rampant, and they felt insecure in an environment that did not have guards as a visible presence. The second-tallest bar amazed them. These homeless students indicated that they needed the school to provide "help with our classwork" much more than any of the things the adults thought they would want. Teachers who had been saying "We're a school, we're here to teach, we can't be a social service agency" discovered that kids felt the same way. They wanted to be taught. The quality improvement project shifted focus from "We're not social workers" to "How can we quickly diagnose their skill levels and provide basic instruction that will move them forward, even if they are only with us a short time?"

Think, Pair, Share

When schools address the "Where are we now?" question, they need to consider their status in terms of student performance, perceptions of school effectiveness, and the organizational climate in which any change process must take place. Histograms, pie charts, and run charts were described as ways to portray student data. The use of surveys, focus groups, and pareto charts to describe stakeholder perceptions was explored. Any of these can also be adapted for analysis of the school culture. Think, Pair, Share is a technique that helps assess the readiness of a school to examine itself and begin to improve.

Purpose. Unlike basic brainstorming, which relies for its value on quick generation of numerous responses without evaluation, Think, Pair, Share is designed to provide a structured opportunity to reflect on a subject before voicing participants' thoughts. Its purpose for the individual participant is to refine and clarify personal viewpoints, prepare rationales to support them, and/or mentally rehearse how to communicate them to others. The purpose for growth of a group is to share opinions honestly and openly, but with greater sensitivity than in an "off-the-cuff" or "already-flown-off-the-handle" confrontation.

When to use. Think, Pair, Share is a helpful technique to raise awareness of concerns or needs for change during the early stages of describing "Where are we now?" As the matrix indicates, it can also be used in many contexts during an improvement process to improve communication and manage conflicts.

Whom to involve. When Think, Pair, Share is used to look at needs for change, all parties involved in the change process should be represented. In the case of school improvement, participants might include members of the site leadership group. When Think, Pair, Share is used for conflict management, participants would be those who are in conflict, or their representatives if large groups are involved.

Materials needed. Think, Pair, Share can be used with no special materials. If common themes emerge during the activity, the facilitator may wish to record them with markers on easel paper or on overhead transparencies.

TIPS FOR FACILITATORS

Give participants a prompt and a time limit of 2-3 minutes to think about it in silence without interaction. Respond to individual learning styles by assuring participants that they may jot down notes or doodle if they so desire as they organize their thoughts. Let them know in advance that they will be asked to share their viewpoints verbally with one other person.

After the "think time" has been provided, have participants pair up and share their viewpoints. In most cases, pairs work best if they are self-selected. However, there may be times when the topic lends itself to structured pairing, such as the Quick-Write example regarding site-based management described in chapter 7. When Think, Pair, Share is used to address areas of conflict, the pairs would consist of a member from each "side" of the issue.

The "sharing time" may be very informal or carefully structured, depending on the topic and composition of the group. In conflict management settings, it may be necessary to structure an uninterrupted time for each participant, as in the active listening exercise described in chapter 7.

After pairs have shared, ask for voluntary comments on what they learned from each other. Exercise your own judgment about whether to record these comments for future reference. Asking "How many other pairs experienced this as well?" and "Shall we make note of it as a common response?" will guide this decision.

FOR EXAMPLE

Metaphors, similes, and analogies make great prompts for Think, Pair, Share. They create strong visual images, encourage creativity, generate humor, and allow concepts to be expressed in a less threatening way than direct dialogue. Think, Pair, Share can provide a wealth of information for diagnosing organizational culture when participants are asked to complete this statement:

If my school were a (choose your own category), it would be a (choose your own example) because _____.

During the sharing time, challenge participants to identify the positive and negative values embedded in the images. The following examples were written by school teams in the United States, Hong Kong, and St. Lucia. They imply strengths and weaknesses of the organizations that can be explored further in group discussions.

If _____ School were an automobile, it would be American made because it has many options and is changing with the times.

If _____ School were a form of entertainment, it would be the Late Night Show because we're No. 1, and we put in a lot of late hours.

If _____ School were literature, it would be an epic poem because of the magnitude, but only the first 12 lines are done and the poets have a long way to go to complete it.

If _____ School were a government, it would be a democracy because everyone votes on everything and now we're gridlocked.

If _____ School were a vacation spot, it would be Wacky Waters because you can choose to get in shallow or deep, there are slippery slides along the way, you get burned if you're not careful, it's popular and crowded, you can go home feeling that you've had a good time, and some folks are just "all wet."

If _____ School were a movie, it would be *The Wizard of Oz* because we never see the man behind the curtain and we're always guessing about what things mean.

If _____ School were a group of animals, it would be horses because most are trainable but some are wild.

A VARIATION

Answering the "Where are we now?" question can sometimes be made easier by asking the related subquestion "How did we get here?" The "think prompt" is to recall significant events in the school's history, including attempted innovations. Participants identify those that were successful or positive and distinguish the factors associated with them that differ from events and changes regarded negatively. The sharing time and reporting to the large group can help diagnose the legacy of change and guide change agents in their approach. Emphasis should be placed on how a new endeavor is similar to a positive change in the past and different from efforts perceived as failures. If, for example, introduction of "the new math" was an "absolute disaster" because "parents didn't have a clue what we were talking about," it is a strong message that communication with the public will be essential to any future innovation.

Flowcharting

Think, Pair, Share provides opportunities to reflect and exchange individual perceptions of the school or district culture. Organizational diagnosis also includes a close look at governance and program factors that reveal how ready the system is to undertake change—whether its routine functions are likely to enhance or inhibit the effort. This is especially true for site-based efforts, which can be well conceived at the building level but crash against insurmountable barriers within the larger organization.

Purpose. Flowcharting is a graphic way to represent steps in a process and relationships between departments or other divisions in an organization. It can be used to illustrate how a process currently works, or to design an ideal process. Sometimes groups try to diagram the current process first to see where it breaks down. Sometimes groups use flowcharting to visualize how the process should take place. On other occasions, the group may divide into two subgroups. One group would draw the current process and the other would try to construct the ideal process to compare the two.

When to use. Flowcharting can be used at the start of a change process to develop a visual plan of the steps that will be needed, critical decision points, and timelines. It can also be used for problem solving whenever an organization senses that its processes are inefficient or redundant.

Whom to involve. When flowcharting is used to create a new process, representatives of all stakeholders should be involved. If flowcharting is used to describe existing processes or to troubleshoot problem areas, people who work with each step of the process should be involved. Trying to flowchart a process without the people who actually participate in it can create ill will that is difficult to overcome in a spirit of constructive criticism and continuous improvement.

Materials needed. Flowcharting can be done using a computer, but most often occurs in small groups using easel paper and markers. Stick-on notes can also be helpful as an intermediate step.

TIPS FOR FACILITATORS

Have the group begin by discussing what it takes to get a process completed, a product created, or a decision approved. The task is to draw each step of the process and connect it with arrows. Simple shapes should be used, such as circles, boxes, and ovals. In some cases, groups will choose a particular shape to represent a certain department or division or group within the organization. One standard rule of thumb is that a diamond shape should be used to represent decision points, where arrows could go in more than one direction based on the decision that is made. If there are more than seven participants, the group should be divided into smaller groups to complete this activity. Do not be concerned if their flowcharts do not turn out the same. A valuable learning occurs when participants realize that even within the organization and as part of the process, they do not have a common understanding of how it works.

FOR EXAMPLE

A middle school had begun to work with site-based management and school improvement. Initial excitement had prompted a number of innovative ideas, but most of them had foundered before implementation because their advocates did not know how to get them approved. The school site council wanted to be sure that any individual or group had the ability to bring forth a new idea and have it receive fair consideration. Members of the council spent several meetings struggling to describe such a process in words or numbered steps. Finally, a frustrated participant exclaimed, "It still doesn't seem clear. Maybe you'd better draw me a picture!" Figure 3.6 is the flowchart that was developed in response.

A VARIATION

As school leadership groups begin to answer the "Where are we now?" question, they sometimes find themselves wondering "How did we get to this state?" The past may need to be revisited, discussed, and laid to rest before the present can be assessed objectively to set new directions. Flowcharting can be useful in this situation as well. The shapes used can represent major events in the history of the school, such as changes of principals, new mandates from the state, shifts in student population, or internal conflicts. The diamond shape used to represent decision points is used to depict turning points, especially if the event caused members of the group to go in different directions. Drawing this type of flowchart can help a group understand the influence of past events and recognize what divisions or rifts may need to be healed during the readiness stage of a change process. When one school team completed flowcharting for this purpose, it discovered that many of the conflicts still being played out among the staff could be traced back 4 years to the district's attempt at implementing a merit pay plan. Once members realized how long they had been carrying old grudges, they made a commitment to bury them and move on.

ANOTHER TWIST

As I worked with a steering committee in one district's boardroom, it became clear that there was a great deal of confusion about how the Quality Task Force fit with the strategic planning process, how the district strategic planning group interacted with the facilities committee, how the school improvement teams fit with parent advocacy groups, and so on. The participants worked diligently to construct a flowchart and finally indicated that flowcharting was much too logical to fit the way things really happened in the district. The variation was to use any type of drawing that would illustrate how they perceived the interaction of these various groups and who they would go to for approval of building-level initiatives. Two drawings were particularly intriguing. One showed a host of colorful balloons, strings dangling, floating haphazardly across a cloudy sky, with

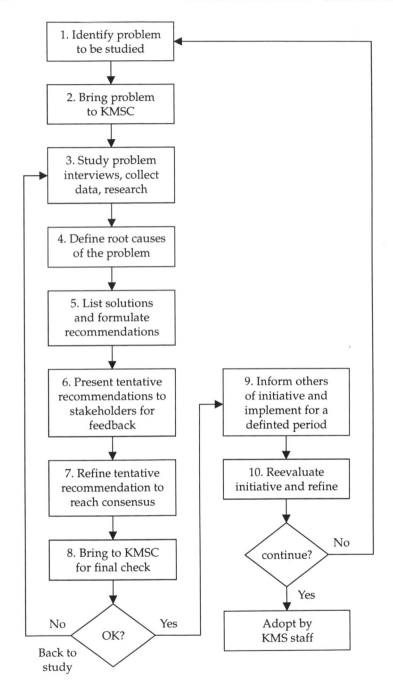

Figure 3.6. Flow Chart for an Initiative

scorch marks on several. The creators of this visual image noted that the district seemed to have a lot of lovely ideas floating around, but that they did not seem connected to anything and that you never knew whether a new idea would soar or be struck by lightning.

Another group created a very complex marionette, with strings attached to ears, eyes, nose, mouth, and limbs. Each of the strings was connected to a different committee or group that it had earlier tried to depict in a flowchart. The artists stated that working on a site-based team in the midst of multiple district efforts felt like being "jerked around" by the conflicting expectations of each entity, none of whom were aware of each others' work. When these two drawings were shared with the superintendent and board president, they clearly demonstrated why the schools could not move forward with site-based leadership until the district reached better consensus and integration of its own projects. Needless to say, the artists remain anonymous.

4

Answering the
"Where Do We Want to Go?"
Question

Travelers and ramblers are different all right. Unfortunately, too many school leadership teams look like the ramblers—"all packed up and no place to go." They've assembled trunkfuls of data and worked frantically to convince their peers that things are really not so good, that they need a change, but they can't get the show on the road because they don't know where they're headed. Larry Lezotte tells school leaders that "if you don't know where you're going, any road will get you there." The problem is that it might be the wrong road, and you might end up in a spot even worse than where you are right now.

The question "Where do we want to go?" is related to the planning stage in the RPTIM model and the plan stage of quality management's PDCA cycle. Leadership teams must generate broad involvement in clarifying and affirming the values of the culture. Semantics of vision or mission and belief statements or philosophy matter little compared to the necessity of building support and commitment to a shared ideal.

The discussion and interaction that take place through the process of drafting a statement of commitment are essential. They open communication, increase interaction, and define a focus for the change process. But the rhetoric of belief statements is unavoidably general and idealistic. The written product is not the sole purpose.

The process of developing it and the even more critical decisions and action taken based on it are the realities that make such activity essential. In or out of vogue, defining beliefs about why we exist is essential as an intrinsic motivator to help sustain a difficult and complex process.

It requires great facilitation skill to move a group toward acceptance of a common belief statement. It requires exceptional creativity to transform general, idealistic rhetoric into something specific and concrete. Identifying the tangible evidence that would be seen, heard, and observed if the ideal became real is an intermediate step that must take place before strategies can be chosen to achieve it.

To answer the question "Where do we want to go?" also requires selection of priorities. The well-planned traveler must make a choice from among a range of attractive destinations. School leaders must set priorities and focus their efforts where they have the greatest likelihood of creating change that lasts. Once these priorities have been established, goals can be set, study groups can identify best practices for meeting them, and progress can be monitored. Processes for building consensus, identifying observable indicators, and establishing priorities are needed to help schools and districts determine "Where do we want to go?"

Affinity Process

When I first learned about mission development, it was taught to me as an "affinity" type of process. Since then, I have seen the term *affinity process* used in quality management literature to describe a process similar to a force field analysis in which pluses and minuses are listed. I have not, however, found a different term to describe the process of combining ideas and topics that have a similarity, or affinity, for one another. If you find my use of the term confusing in light of your prior knowledge, feel free to change it here and on the matrix in chapter 1 for your personal use.

Purpose. This process is designed to help people with different values find those they hold in common. These common ideals are then put into writing and consensus is built so they become the guiding criteria in decision making and planning.

When to use. The most common use of this process is when a school or district is just beginning to examine itself and accept its responsibility for continuous improvement. To successfully answer the question "Where do we want to go?" an organization must identify a destination that's worth the trip. When a journey becomes difficult, it is harder to quit if the arrival is strongly desired by the travelers.

A process like this can also be helpful whenever an organization seems to be lacking focus. It should be repeated periodically to reaffirm that the same beliefs are still valued, refine them as needed in terms of changes in the environment, and socialize new members of the organization.

Whom to involve. "The more the merrier"—or at least the more effective. Widespread involvement from all stakeholder groups is needed if the statement of commitment is to drive decision making and change. Sometimes I hear statements like "Yes, we have a mission statement but it doesn't mean a thing and no one knows what it is." A few probing questions usually reveal that the mission statement was written by an individual (the new principal?) or by a small group "on retreat" and delivered as a product. Although it is the responsibility of a leader to shape a culture and reinforce positive norms, I have never forgotten this advice from Bob Garmston: "My content is not as important as their process."

Materials needed. The most expensive resources for this process are the human resources to facilitate it and the time that it requires to allow adequate involvement but move it along swiftly enough that it does not get bogged down. The number of stakeholder groups and the numbers of constituents from each group who wish to participate will influence the time factor. Concrete materials needed are stick-on notes, construction paper, and chart paper. A room with a large, blank wall allows the activity to take the most concrete, tangible form.

TIPS FOR FACILITATORS

This process has been successfully accomplished with groups up to 100 when divided into small subgroups for appropriate steps. First, ask participants to reflect silently about one or more prompts that are visually displayed. What is the purpose of this school? What should it accomplish for its students? What characteristics should make this school stand out from other schools? What function is uniquely ours to accomplish?

Tell them to work **independently** and write each idea on a stick-on note. Urge them to use no more than five or six words to convey a thought. Caution them not to include more than one idea on each sheet. Guide them to use positive phrases to communicate the role of the school.

The next step is to form **small groups.** These may be mixed groups of school staff, parents, and other stakeholders, or they may be small groups based on role. Composition of the groups is a judgment call on the part of the facilitator, who should learn as much as possible about the history and culture of the school before accepting this responsibility. If there is great interest in participation, the initial steps of the process may be repeated at several meetings to give everyone a chance for input.

At each table, one person should introduce an idea he or she has recorded and ask others if they have something similar. These stick-on notes should be attached to a sheet of paper. The next person around the table should introduce one of his or her ideas, ask for similar responses, and compile them on another sheet of paper. This affinity process should be repeated until participants have joined all their phrases with those of other group members.

For the next step, tell the groups to look at each sheet of stick-on notes and create a three- to five-word heading that expresses the main point or theme. Once the small groups have arrived at headings for their clusters, reassemble as a **whole group.** Ask one group to bring a heading sheet and post it on the wall. Repeat a similar process of asking other groups to add theirs with similar items. Continue combining sheets of notes until all work is posted.

Return to **small groups** to discuss which concepts they feel are most important and what wording they see that best expresses the underlying thought. They may appreciate a sample advocacy statement ("I like this phrase because it communicates that . . .") to help them describe their preferences in a positive manner.

Charge each small group with drafting a very rough statement that uses the short headings it chose to most accurately convey its members' thoughts. If these rough drafts are completed in the same setting (such as a workshop), have them shared with the **whole**

group. If the steps so far have been conducted in an afterschool or evening meeting, the small groups can finish their rough drafts and then submit them to the **leadership team.**

When the leadership team has received input from the groups at the workshop or from a series of meetings with stakeholder groups, it begins to synthesize the main ideas from the various products and prepares a complete draft. This draft should be disseminated to **all individuals or groups** who participated in the first set of drafts. It is important to create opportunities for them to have discussion and provide direct feedback to the team, not just return the draft with written comments.

The **leadership team** uses the feedback to further revise the statement or document, but completion of the written product is not the end of the team's work. The mission or set of belief statements will only guide the organization if it is consciously and overtly introduced as a central focus for all future decision making. The leadership team should plan a very visible celebration and commitment event. Some schools have held signing ceremonies complete with special pens to commemorate the occasion. **All groups** who contributed to the process should participate in this public event. When the celebration is over, the **leadership team** has an ongoing responsibility to plan ways of infusing the mission into all decision-making processes and into the culture of the school. The team may identify a subgroup or a small, separate committee and charge it to be "keeper of the vision."

Creating the statement of commitment is just the first small step in identifying what the school wants to create, the destination it seeks in response to "Where do we want to go?" Referencing and reaffirming the mission of the school throughout the change process will move it "off the wall" and "into the walk" of daily routines and practices. School leaders must challenge the organization on a regular basis with application questions like "What are we doing to support our mission? Which of our current programs and practices are consistent with the values we espouse? Which aren't? Are the things we measure and assess the things that we say are truly important?" One of the school leadership team's responsibilities is to plan activities that will consciously and intentionally inculcate the school's values into its cultural norms. Some ways to continually affirm the values of the organization are discussed in chapter 7.

FOR EXAMPLE

The following mission statements were developed through the process described above. They are clear and concise, strongly worded, and convey a sense of the organization's responsibility to accomplish them.

> The staff of _____ School believes that *all* students can learn and can achieve mastery of basic grade-level skills, regardless of their previous academic performance, family background, socioeconomic status, race, or gender. We believe that our school's purpose is to educate all students to high levels of academic performance while fostering positive growth in social and emotional behaviors and attitudes. We accept the responsibility to teach all students so that they can attain their maximum educational potential.

> The mission of _____ is to help students acquire the knowledge, skills, and attitudes necessary to become healthy, happy, productive adults; to help students become enthusiastic lifelong learners who are able to manage change; and to help students to perpetuate and improve the democratic process and have an impact on their communities, their country, and the world.

> _____ Schools will create an accountable learning community that encourages all students to achieve, to their highest potential, the knowledge and skills needed to be fulfilled, productive members of a changing society.

A SIDE NOTE

In the group process described earlier, bold print was used to identify the roles of individuals, small groups, the whole group, and the leadership team. The expansion and contraction from individual work to small groups to large groups and back to small groups may be visualized with the metaphor of playing an accordion. The leadership team orchestrates the movements of the accordion. The more support it will need to accomplish a task, the more it will need to expand the accordion and bring in a greater volume of air and energy.

Brainstorming

Too often the intense involvement of developing a commitment statement or set of beliefs has no impact because it does not direct the action of the organization. It's like a rambler saying "I'd sure love to take the perfect vacation" without determining what criteria would make a vacation "perfect." Travelers, on the other hand, are more likely to say, "The perfect vacation spot would be quiet, isolated, with lots of sunshine, moderate temperatures, and hiking trails."

Purpose. The purpose of brainstorming is to generate as many ideas as possible related to a particular problem, issue, or goal. It is not tied to current reality, as were the processes described in chapter 3. Brainstorming is designed to add new ideas to the status quo.

When to use. The number of Xs on the matrix makes it clear that brainstorming is a very versatile group process that can be used for many reasons at almost any point in a change process. It is described here as a follow-up phase after affirming the values of an organization. The specific purpose and timing are to make the mission more concrete by identifying observable indicators that would prove the mission was being accomplished.

Whom to involve. Active participation by a broad range of constituents from all stakeholder groups was recommended for affirming the value system of the organization. Smaller groups with an understanding of the educational enterprise will be better able to contribute to this phase.

Materials needed. Brainstorming requires open minds, markers, and poster paper.

Tips for Facilitators
Describe the rules of brainstorming to participants:

- Quantity is more important than quality.
- Share every thought that occurs to you.
- Make no evaluative statements.
- Listen carefully to group members.

Focus the brainstorming on the problem or purpose. When addressing the "Where do we want to go?" question, the need is to focus on the concrete, tangible evidence we could see and hear if an organization were living by its beliefs. A helpful phrase to use with groups is "observable indicators." This phrase acknowledges that some important aspects of school life are not measurable in the traditional sense of a quantified assessment, but should be observed in the behavior of its members.

Record every idea that is expressed, in the words of the speaker. Do not edit or combine with others you think are the same. Set a time limit of 10-15 minutes to create a sense of urgency. Within that time period, be comfortable with moments of silence. The next contributions are usually even more creative and insightful than those before the pause.

FOR EXAMPLE

The mission statement was brand new. It included phrases about basic skills, responsible citizenship, and respect. The school leadership team felt quite confident about writing goals and action plans consistent with those ideals. But the members were stumped by the phrase "lifelong learner." How would they incorporate that into their improvement plans and verify whether they accomplished it? One member sardonically remarked, "Yeah, right! Now our postgraduation follow-up studies have to track them down at age 70!"

The prebrainstorming challenge was to first think individually of someone each person considered to be a lifelong learner. The brainstorming task was to list what they had seen that person do, or heard that person say, that convinced them she or he was a lifelong learner. The list included items like "gets interested in something," "goes to the library to find out more about it," "is open to do new things," "starts projects on her own," "tries to get other people interested," "keeps after it until he knows all there is to know and then is on to something else," and "likes to figure out her own way to do it." It was a fascinating list, but the group wondered how helpful it would be because they were describing adults.

The next challenge was a variation on the same theme. Based on the age of the students they parented or taught, smaller groups were formed and challenged to brainstorm "What does each of those behaviors look like at age 17? at age 11? at age 7?" This second round of brainstorming yielded two sets of results. One was the conclusion that most of those behaviors looked pretty much the same at any age and could be observed in the school setting. The other was a realization that many of the school's practices in grouping and scheduling limited a student's ability to demonstrate those behaviors.

Brainstorming is useful in the "Where do we want to go?" stage to set some criteria that distinguish the desired state from the status quo. These criteria also become factors to assess as the group monitors its progress.

Nominal Group Process

A mission statement helps describe where the organization wants to go, and brainstorming observable indicators generates criteria to make the statement more concrete. A third important part of answering this question is setting priorities for improvement.

Purpose. In spite of general agreement about what the school should accomplish for its students, there is still a wide range of viewpoints about which aspects of the school should be improved to do so more effectively. Nominal group process gives everyone an opportunity to participate in selecting which areas to work on first.

When to use. Because it is never possible to address everyone's concerns about the school, nominal group process is used in the planning stage to select priorities. It can also be used to reach consensus on other important decisions throughout a change process. The nominal group technique is particularly helpful in situations where powerful individuals have a habit of dominating discussions and where "competing for air time" has been the prevailing way of gaining influence.

Whom to involve. All interested parties should be invited to participate. They must be made aware that nominal group technique will be used and that it is a structured process designed (and tested and proven effective) to allow an equal voice for all participants.

Materials needed. The sequence of steps and rules for nominal group process should be posted. The facilitator will need markers, poster paper, an easel, and tape. Index cards or stick-on notes will help participants with their ranking.

Post and provide an overview of these steps before beginning:

- Individual brainstorming
- Round-robin listing
- Individual ranking of priorities
- Tabulation of ranks
- Discussion
- Individual ranking
- Tabulation of ranks

Call attention to the fact that "discussion" is far down the list and that this is by design. The sequence was developed to provide an opportunity for all ideas to be generated and included through brainstorming and to encourage individual reflection and decision making before group members begin to influence each other.

Stimulate the **individual brainstorming** step by posing a question like "What are all the things that anyone might say could be improved about our school?" As the question is displayed, underline the word *all* and emphasize that this is their opportunity to create a comprehensive list for consideration and that they should be candid and list every concern they have. Call attention to the word *anyone* and remind them to present not only their viewpoints but others of which they are aware. This is an opportune time to review results of survey data and be sure the concerns of constituents are included, even if they are not present to participate. Stress that the word *could* expresses our commitment to continuous improvement and does not imply that the current situation is abysmal. Groups are often reassured and encouraged to be open by the statement that "when we talk about improvement, we're not thinking 'horrible-to-wonderful.' We're thinking 'good-better-best.' "

Observe the individual brainstorming and allow plenty of time until most participants seem to be done writing. Emphasize that every one of their concerns will be included but that it will be helpful if they look over them to be sure they are specific and easily understood. Suggest that longer statements be reduced to a short three- to five-word phrase. Mention that a concern like "student test scores" will be more helpful if it is broken down into more specifics like "reading achievement" or "math problem solving." Even if that makes their list longer, it is good to subdivide such general items because reading scores and math scores would be approached differently if they became the school's goals.

If the group consists of 15 or fewer participants, serve as recorder and conduct the **round-robin listing** step of the process. If you are working with a large group, divide it into smaller units and have them select a recorder. If a group member becomes recorder, she can give her list to another participant who will be sure that items from both lists are included.

Round-robin listing means that each person states one concern from his or her list, and this is repeated around the circle. Emphasize that everyone must listen carefully and cross things off the list that other people mention to avoid duplication and keep the process moving quickly. The recorder should assign a letter to each item (see For Example) to facilitate ranking and discussion later.

If you have facilitated a small group, you now have one list of all concerns. If you divided a large group into smaller groups who actually represented different schools, each group has it own total list and will rank those items. However, if everyone in a large group was from the same school, you need to take a break and combine the separate group lists into a total master list. This can be done quickly during a break for the large group, either by repeating the round-robin exercise or by word processing all the responses and then printing the master list for each participant.

When the list of "all the things that could be improved" has been completed, give each person five index cards or slips of paper. Direct them to choose the five items they are most concerned about, and put the letter of each one on a separate slip. If a group member is most concerned about the items labeled *A, E, J, M,* and *P,* there would now be a card or slip of paper with a letter *A,* another with *E,* a third with *J,* and so forth. Then tell the group it must further prioritize the items by shuffling them around until the most important concern is at the top, and the other four are lying on the table, or held in the hand in descending order. The group should then put a number 5 on the top one, a 4 on the next, and so on down to 1. These directions must be very clear, and you should check to see that they are being followed correctly. If you do not check them, some participants will **rank** their concerns in reverse order from the rest of the group. A value of five should represent their top priority, so that the highest total represents the greatest concern when all are compiled.

When they have ranked their items, they should rearrange their cards in alphabetical order. The recorder may call out a letter, and each person who ranked it states the numerical value he or she gave it. The recorder should write down each ranking, rather than just add them mentally and record a total. When discussion takes place, it will make a difference whether one concern has a total value of 20 because ten people ranked it a 2 or because four people ranked it a 5.

Discussion begins after the rankings have been tabulated. By this time, almost every group can see agreement beginning to emerge around top-priority concerns. In some cases, a second round of **ranking** and **tabulating** is unnecessary because the priorities become very clear and the discussion does not indicate any strong disagreement with them. If there is disagreement or if questions are raised about some items, ask if those who "gave it a 5" would share their reasons for being so concerned about it. Sometimes their responses will provide new information for other participants and cause them to shift their priorities. On other occasions, questions will raise the need for more accurate information before a final decision is reached. In this situation, help the group decide what information is needed, who can provide it, and how much time will be needed to get the information. Then schedule another meeting to look at the information before a second round of ranking determines the school's priorities.

FOR EXAMPLE

The charts generated by one team looked like this:

A.	Classroom management	5, 5, 1, 3, 5, 4	23
B.	Teacher punctuality	—	—
C.	Parental involvement	2, 5	7
D.	Time on task	5, 4, 2	11
E.	Teacher motivation	3	3
F.	Community participation	—	—
G.	Student evaluation	4, 3, 5, 5, 1	18
H.	Physical environment	—	—
I.	Quality of instruction	2, 4, 4, 5, 4, 5	24
J.	Teacher evaluation	4, 3	7
K.	Discipline	—	—
L.	Student involvement	—	—
M.	Pupil-teacher rapport	3	3
N.	Interpersonal relationships	2	2
O.	Staff development	3, 3, 2, 3, 2	13
P.	Cocurricular activities	1	1
Q.	Principal-teacher relations	—	—

R.	Teacher involvement in curriculum development	—	—
S.	Instructional leadership	5, 4, 5	14
T.	Staff supervision	2, 2, 1, 1	6
U.	Communication	—	—
V.	School's curriculum	—	—
W.	Student motivation	—	—
X.	Staffing configuration	—	—
Y.	Empowerment	—	—
Z.	Homework policy	—	—
AA.	Instructional materials	—	—
BB.	Grant writing	—	—

Completion of the nominal group process focused the school on the quality of instruction, classroom management, and student evaluation. Goals were written for each of these concerns. The interest in staff development did not surface as one of the top priorities, but its presence in the list encouraged the district to offer workshops related to the three goal areas that emerged.

A VARIATION

The nominal group process is a good way to give all participants an equal voice in setting priorities. However, there is a weakness inherent in starting with brainstorming. Too often, members of the group contribute concerns that arise only from their personal awareness. Sometimes the priorities that emerge have little connection with the beliefs that the school or district has created as its ideals. Of even greater concern is the omission of concerns that were revealed by the data analysis done in response to the "Where are we now?" question.

A variation is to schedule a review of the statement of commitment and a short summary of the findings of the data shortly before the meeting at which the nominal group process will be conducted. Urge those who attend this review to think about the findings and participate in setting priorities for improvement. On a smaller scale, the facilitator may remind the group to think briefly about the organization's values and the data summaries that have been available for study. Urge them to include that information as they list areas of concern.

The influence of data on the priorities and direction of school improvement plans became obvious to me in a large district that I visited several times. On each trip, I provided school improvement training to a different group of school teams. Data from statewide assessments became available midway through this multiphase training effort.

Priority concerns identified by nine schools *before* state test data were received are listed below. (The list totals more than nine because each school chose from two to five goals.)

Student attendance	3
Teacher attendance	3
Reading achievement	2
Student discipline	2
Home-school communication	2
Parent involvement	2
Math achievement	1
Quality of teaching	1
Minority achievement gap	1
Meaningful staff development	1
Student motivation	1
Parent commitment	1
Teacher commitment	1
Internal school communication	1

Priority concerns identified by nine similar schools *after* state test data were received by the district are as follows:

Reading achievement	8
Math achievement	5
Attendance	3
Student discipline	2
Parent involvement	1
Curriculum planning	1
Conflict resolution	1
Time to "do all this"	1
Home-school relations	1
Team functioning	1
Closing minority gap	1
Writing achievement	1
Staff buy-in	1
Student self-esteem	1

Eight of the nine teams who had test data before them and had reviewed the data prior to goal setting focused their priorities on student achievement, compared with two of nine that had not considered test data before the goal-setting activities.

Color Coding

Color coding is not so much a group process as a way of identifying the sources of responses. In chapter 3, printing surveys on different-colored sheets of paper was described as a way to be sure that results include representation from all groups or neighborhoods. If separate meetings are held for various stakeholders to participate in the mission development process, different colors of stick-on notes can be used at each session. As responses are grouped, a visual scan can help assure that contributions from all groups are included in the final product. Color coding can also be used when activities like the nominal group process are conducted to establish priorities.

Purpose. The purpose of color coding is to show which concerns or priorities are of most interest to which participants. This information may help school leaders find interested people to help with change efforts. It can also highlight concerns that may need informal attention, even though they do not emerge as the shared priorities of the overall group.

When to use. Use color coding when there may be more than one set of priorities, or when more than one set of volunteers may be needed to carry out a series of tasks.

Whom to involve. It is repetitious, but important, to note again that all who may be affected by a change, or expected to help assist with its implementation, should be included in determining the priorities.

Materials needed. The facilitators will need chart paper, markers, and tape. Each participant will need a predetermined number of colored stickers or stars. The number of colors needed will depend on the range of constituent groups participating in the process.

Use brainstorming to generate the list of concerns or problems that participants feel should be addressed. This step is the same as the beginning of the nominal group technique, but the rest of the process is less formal. After the list of items has been recorded on large chart paper, be sure that each participant has five dots or stars of the appropriate color. Participants go to the charts and place their five dots or stars by the five items they consider to be top priorities for most immediate attention.

FOR EXAMPLE

The district had been without a curriculum director for several months. Even before that, work on instructional programs and assessment had virtually ground to a halt because of budget cuts. An interim administrator was assigned to determine the areas that most needed attention and to set up a timeline for addressing them as funds became available. Because the district no longer had curriculum specialists, these assignments had been divided among the principals in addition to their building-level responsibilities. A method was needed for setting priorities in order and organizing work on them in the most efficient manner.

The first step was to brainstorm the list of issues and projects that had been neglected and needed attention. Once the list was complete, central office administrators were given five gold dots, secondary principals were given five purple dots, and elementary principals were given five green dots. A quick visual scan of their responses identified two issues that had multicolored responses and would be handled in a K-12 setting. Other issues that had only purple or green dots could be set aside to be addressed in subcommittees that were just secondary or elementary in composition. A few issues remained on the list for attention at some future date, but the delay would not cause any hurt feelings because the items had no preponderance of dots of any color.

Weighted Voting

Color coding helps show differences in the priorities set by different individuals or groups. Weighted voting is somewhat different.

Through weighted voting, participants can show the relative value they place on different issues. They can show that they feel more strongly about some concerns than others.

Purpose. Weighted voting provides a measure of the relative importance placed on various items by individuals and groups.

When to use. Use weighted voting when "not all items are created equal" in the eyes of the participants. If a participant in the color-coding activity had said, "Can I put all my five dots on just one thing?" it would have been a signal that weighted voting could be used.

Whom to involve. The same people who would have been part of the other priority-setting activities would also be involved in weighted voting. This process is particularly appropriate when the participants will bear primary responsibility for the tasks that are identified. It gives them a greater opportunity to determine where they will invest their energies.

Materials needed. The facilitator will need chart paper, markers, and tape. Each participant will need a predetermined number of dots, stickers, or labels, but they may all be the same color.

TIPS FOR FACILITATORS

Start by having participants brainstorm the issues to be addressed or the tasks to be done, in the same way that the nominal group process began. As in color coding, the participants have five dots or stickers. The uniqueness of weighted voting is that they may distribute their five dots (or votes) in any combination. If they feel that one item is crucial for immediate attention, they can use all five of their dots to indicate its importance. If they want to be sure that attention is given to two items, they may use two dots for one and three for the other. Depending on the number of participants and length of the brainstormed list, the facilitator may allocate more or less than five votes per participant.

FOR EXAMPLE

They had been teaching all day, it was hot, and the room had no windows. Because of budget cuts, the schools were not allowed to hire subs for professional development activities, so we were going to meet from 4:00 to 7:00 on three consecutive evenings. It was precious time and the people donating it to learn how to function as a school leadership team were precious too. Meeting their needs and making the content relevant were essential—but it was clear that they came with a range of expectations so varied that it could not possibly be addressed in 9 hours of less-than-prime learning time. The challenge was to focus the agenda in some way that would clearly show respect for their time and priorities. Knowing we could not include them all, we listed the topics they had anticipated and gave five stars to each participant. As they left the first evening session, they placed their stars on the list to express their priorities. The results looked like this:

Selecting strategies related to curriculum	*****************
Process used to develop implementation plan	*********************************
Timelines	**********
Moving from departmentalized to multidisciplinary	********
Team skills	*********************************
Strengthening our belief system	************
How to use data in decision making	*******************
Ways to gather data	********************************
Motivating students with no role models or hope	******************************** ******************************** ****************
Difference between making easy and hard changes	**********
How to avoid bandwagons	*******************
Difference between school improvement and strategic planning	***

It was clear that the strongest interest of the participants related to student motivation, which was no part of the planned training. Fortunately, the next set of priorities (development of action plans combined with timelines, teamwork skills, and gathering and using data) was part of the planned agenda. I was able to focus on those topics while having my materials on student motivation Express Mailed to me for the last session. Participation in the weighted voting activity created a high level of commitment that overcame the poor timing and conditions. Because they could see the needs expressed by the whole group, those whose topics were omitted understood and accepted that result.

One comment on the evaluation sheet read, "This is the first time I've felt like I had some control over what we did in a workshop. I didn't mind the evenings, because I was getting what I came for." One way to turn ramblers into travelers is by using group process techniques to help them shape their own destination as you address the question "Where do we want to go?"

5

Answering the "How Will We Get There?" Question

An ancient proverb reads "The journey of a thousand miles begins with a single step." Too many school change efforts go nowhere because the leaders confuse choosing the destination or goal with having a plan. Although change processes must be flexible enough and adjusted often enough to be considered evolutionary, the initial implementation plan must be specific enough to identify what that first single step is.

Development of a plan or map for the journey blends planning, training, and implementation aspects of the RPTIM model. Training is needed in how to plan, and the plan will include needs for training about best practices and how to implement appropriate strategies. In the PDCA cycle of quality management, answering the "How will we get there?" question is the planning stage. In the *Three Is* model, this phase may include implementation of the shared decision-making aspect of change, whereas specific strategies to improve the school or district are still being identified for initiation.

Addressing the "How will we get there?" question requires organizations to be honest about why they are not there yet. That includes identifying factors that contribute to the disparity between the desired situation and the actual situation described as "Where are we now?" It also requires schools and districts to accept responsibility for those factors that are within their control and match their stated mission. The cause-and-effect (fishbone) process assists school leaders with those challenges.

For an improvement plan to be successful, it must be developed with awareness of the barriers that need to be overcome. Force field analysis is a useful tool for identifying these potential obstacles.

For any problem, there are multiple solutions, and organizations like schools that have limited resources and high visibility need to choose those most likely to produce the intended results. Use of a decision matrix improves choices of strategies. When answers to the subquestions "Why aren't we there yet?" "What factors can we affect?" and "What strategies shall we use?" have been found, development of the action plan is relatively simple. Identify specific steps, decide who will be involved and who will take primary responsibility, determine what resources will be needed and how to acquire them, set a timeline based on realistic estimates, and above all, select the indicators that will prove progress is being made. Easier said than done!

Cause-and-Effect Diagram (Fishbone)

A cause-and-effect diagram is a visual representation of the relationships between contributing factors and an issue or problem. Because the picture usually branches out like the skeleton of a fish, it has come to be known as a "fishbone."

Purpose. A cause-and-effect diagram is helpful when groups need to better understand why a problem situation exists and how it developed. This information can help teams identify the factors with the most impact and choose the most promising entry points for interventions.

When to use. The cause-and-effect diagramming process is very helpful when groups have agreed that a specific issue or problem should be the focus of planning and change. It can also be a useful tool in conflict management by providing greater understanding of factors that have contributed to the conflict situation.

Whom to involve. Any of the stakeholders who have been identified earlier may be involved in small groups to develop cause-and-effect diagrams and share their product and insights with others. It has been my experience that this group process is one uniquely suited to groups that include skeptics. The example that follows demonstrates how it can defuse some of their resistance by acknowledging that many of the causal factors are beyond the control of the school, and can help shift their perspective from negatives to possibilities.

Materials needed. Completing a cause-and-effect diagram is a simple paper-and-pencil process. If small groups will be reporting to a larger group, easel paper and markers should be used.

TIPS FOR FACILITATORS

Explain to the group that before we leap to decisions about how to solve a problem, we need to be sure we understand it thoroughly. This activity will help us look back for causes before we look forward with plans. Have groups state the problem they are addressing in a simple phrase such as "student absenteeism" or "lack of problem-solving skills." The phrase should be written in a box (or the artistic may draw a fishhead instead) halfway down the right-hand side of a large horizontal sheet of paper. A line should be drawn across the middle of the paper, like a spine leading to the head of the fish. As the groups brainstorm the factors that contribute to their concern, they write each one on a diagonal "bone" attached to the spine, or on a "barb" connected to a bone if it relates to a cause already mentioned.

Some formal group process handbooks emphasize that causal factors tend to fall into categories and that the categories should be identified first and bones attached to the appropriate category. For example, quality management fishbones often include the four categories of procedures, people, policies, and plant. Having seen too many groups get bogged down deciding what the categories should be, or arguing about which category a factor belongs with, I have left the process unstructured. It seems to be just as effective without the predetermined categories. In fact, some groups recognize their own categories after working a while and revise their fishbone accordingly.

A version of the quality improvement technique of "Ask why five times" can strengthen the fishbone exercise. When a contributing factor is identified, the repeated question "And where did that one come from?" or "And why is that?" can add more specificity to the analysis.

After the cause-and-effect diagram is drawn and discussed, guide the group to identify any follow-up steps. Factors over which the organization has no control may be acknowledged. There may be a need to gather more data on some of the factors, to see how much influence they actually have. Most important, the group should star or circle causes it feels have great impact and that it is willing to address.

FOR EXAMPLE

Ten school leadership teams had been selected to participate in a 3-day workshop that would guide them through the process of developing a school improvement plan. They had been asked to bring student data and draft versions of any work they had already done on mission statements, goals, or action plans. Their approach to the workshop setting was fascinating in and of itself.

At one table sat a group of newspapers—at least, that's what it looked like. All I could see were the open sports sections of *USA Today* and local and state publications.

At another table, a group of early arrivals were poring over a stack of computer printouts, heedless even of the caterer's late delivery of the pastries. Heads together, the participants were engrossed in a discussion of which subtests matched their curriculum and mission closely enough to merit major attention as they set their improvement targets.

Another group entered carrying the lid of a copy paper box with waves of green-and-white-striped computer printouts spilling haphazardly over the edge. Locating the table with the school's name on it, the carrier dropped the box onto the floor and used the side of his foot to slide it—none too gently—under the table out of sight. Having dispatched the data, this group attacked the coffee and doughnut table with much greater zeal. I overheard one say, "So what's with this woman we have to listen to from Effective Schools? Who had the nerve to decide we were defective?"

It was already shaping up to be one of those marvelous "opportunity days," like the tough games that some coaches refer to as character-builders, when one of the speaker's companions approached me. "In all fairness, I really ought to let you know that there's no reason for us to be wasting 3 days at this workshop. We already have our school improvement plan done." Swallowing hard, I asked him to tell me what they had planned for the coming year. "Well, we got our biggest problem figured out. It's kids not coming to school. And we got two plans for working on it. First of all, we got a business partner that's going to donate us some equipment so we can program it to call those kids and get them going in the morning. Second of all, we got a committee all lined up to work on our attendance policy so these kids can't get by with skipping. Anything wrong with that?" By now I was *gulping* hard, but I managed to thank him for his honesty and suggested they stick it out for at least this first day, listen carefully, and think about their plan, and we'd talk at the end of the day about whether their attendance at the next 2 would be worthwhile. "Well, I guess we might as well, we're already here."

During the first part of the morning, I shared some background on effective schools research with the group. When we did carousel brainstorming to record their impressions of the correlates identified by Edmonds and Lezotte, I praised this group for addressing attendance, linking it with orderly environment, high expectations for students, and opportunity to learn. I assured my new friend that they were exactly right—kids aren't going to learn if they're not even there.

Later, I asked them to talk about whatever data they had available and what concerns emerged from this discussion or others that had already taken place at their school. This group repeated that their attendance data showed a need for improvement.

Lunch was provided in the room right next door, so I figured this group would stick around for the afternoon. That's when we got to discuss how important it is to understand the problem we're addressing and know just what is causing it so we know where to begin changing it. The group in question began its fishbone of student absenteeism with "parents don't care" and went right on to list items like "no transportation," "baby-sitting younger kids," "pretty low socioeconomics," and "stay up too late at their night jobs." The other groups were getting along well, so I tried to coach this group a little. I commented, "You seem to have a pretty good handle on their family situation. Got any thoughts about the kids themselves?" The next phase started with "kids don't care either," "unmotivated" (when they have night jobs?), and went on to "discipline problems," "low achievers," and "a couple of them are pregnant." About this time, I noticed one member of the group sort of digging around under the table, but it had a skirt around it and I didn't want to get too nosy, so I ignored him.

The work on the fishbone was bogging down, so I tried again. "It's really too bad some kids are like that, but I'm glad to see you're aware of them. Could there be any other source of factors that relates to whether kids come to school or not?" A soft voice from the other end of the table said, "Well, they don't like school when they do come." Several people just stared at her, so I reached over and wrote "don't like school" on a new bone. A few others added things like "don't participate in anything," "can't see the point of learning," and "don't seem connected to anyone."

Just then, a head popped up with the copy paper box lid in his hand and an expression of amazement on his face. "Wait a minute. I've just been digging through here and it looks to me like there's about 20 kids or so in the whole school that are causing our absence rate to look so bad." My friend responded immediately. "Oh, yeah. So *who?*" As the analyst mentioned a name or two, other members of the group began to comment on the individuals. "Well, if _____ can just make it from the bus to the door without a fight, he does pretty well in class." "_____ doesn't have any trouble getting here, but he's so interested in messing around the art room he doesn't follow his schedule." "If _____ wasn't so worried about her weight, she might have time to think about her work."

Because of a little data, the participants suddenly began to talk about students. And as they did, one brave soul said, "You know, if they are so low SES, do you think they'll have phones to call?" Another drew courage from that colleague and said, "If they really don't care about school, what good will a new attendance policy do?" My friend shrugged and said, "Well, maybe our plan isn't quite right, but look at the stuff on that fish-thing. We can't do anything about that stuff." I was delighted. "You're right, you know. I have to agree with you that a lot of these things we can't control. Let's put a check mark by them. And then let's see what we can tackle."

Figure 5.1 shows the results. Not too many items got checked off, because some members of the group began to argue that maybe the system *could* make some kind of provisions for transportation and in-school child care. What they circled became the basis of a new action plan.

The next morning they got there first. By the end of the day, they had developed a plan that would provide each of the chronic absentees with an adult in the school (teacher, custodian, volunteer) who would check in with them each morning before school and follow up to see if they were taking work home afterward.

The next fall, I asked my contact in that district how the teams were getting along and what progress the members had made on their plans. "Well," he said, "they're all making progress but only one

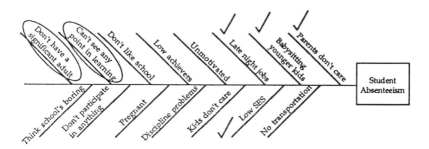

Figure 5.1. Cause-and-Effect (Fishbone) Diagram of Student Absenteeism

school is really implementing what they talked about in June." Care to guess which team it was?

Force Field Analysis

The cause-and-effect diagram helps groups identify the factors contributing to their problem or concern. Force field analysis goes a step further, looking at factors that work both for and against the desired result.

Purpose. Force field analysis is used to identify barriers that must be overcome and to focus on positive forces that can be mobilized for progress.

When to use. Use force field analysis when a group is considering a change effort. The results can help the members be more aware of barriers they didn't recognize. It can also increase a group's sense of efficacy by identifying advantages and possible allies that could help it succeed. Occasionally, time spent doing a force field analysis saves a group from investing time and effort where restraining forces so outweigh driving forces that it's clearly a lost cause from the outset.

Whom to involve. All stakeholders should feel welcome to participate directly or through their representatives on the leadership team or task force. It is particularly important to include those who were strong voices in identifying the issue or problem under consideration.

Materials needed. Force field analysis is a paper-and-pencil exercise. Using easel paper and markers makes it easier to share the completed analysis with others.

TIPS FOR FACILITATORS

Force field analysis is simply a structured version of brainstorming with a format provided for responses. The rules of brainstorming should be reviewed. Like the cause-and-effect diagram, it is important to push the participants beyond "filling in the blanks" to selecting which restraining forces they can minimize and which driving forces they will use. Strategies will emerge from this discussion that can be further developed as part of the action plan.

FOR EXAMPLE

An inner-city-school team was concerned about the gap created in children's lives between May and September and had spent considerable time discussing and debating the value of year-round school. Most members agreed that it was a good concept but wondered if it was feasible to focus their school improvement efforts around restructuring of the school calendar. They decided to complete a force field analysis and "calculate the odds" before going any further. Figure 5.2 shows their analysis.

After looking at it, they decided to work on summer provisions in collaboration with social service agencies and focus their grant funding toward those efforts. They concluded that their resources would get to children much quicker this way than by trying to influence the district, state, county, and parents in favor of year-round school.

Decision Matrix

From my study window, I look up at the Horsetooth, a rock formation on the front range of the Colorado Rockies. To get from here to Estes Park and over the top to Granby, there is really only one route, the Trail Ridge Road. But the view from the deck in back is different. The high plains stretch as far as the eye can see. To get from here to Minneapolis, there are several routes. Having a clear destina-

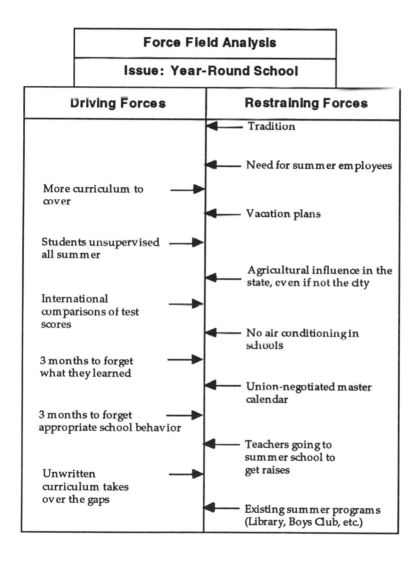

Figure 5.2. Force Field Analysis for Year-Round School

tion does not complete the planning. If there are many possible routes, choices must be made that will get the most people on board and headed in the same direction.

Purpose. A decision matrix is used to help groups reach consensus on the best solution to a complex issue or problem. Choosing criteria that would define an appropriate strategy helps participants focus on common values. Brainstorming all possible solutions brings out greater creativity and can counteract the "only one right or best way" thinking that is so prevalent.

When to use. A decision matrix is helpful when multiple strategies have been suggested, especially if there are intense feelings about several of them. It should definitely be used when organizations have a history of simply adopting the latest innovation and assuming it will match their needs, or when they show little evidence of connecting their data and their value system to decision making. Use of the decision matrix should have been preceded by study of the organization's own data (Where are we now?) and study of best practices for achieving the results desired (Where do we want to go?).

Whom to involve. Group processes should be open for participation. When using a decision matrix, it is particularly important to include those who are most affected by the current situation and those who will be most responsible for implementing the chosen strategies.

Materials needed. Chart paper and markers will be needed for the first two steps. Each participant will need a copy of the decision matrix. There are two ways of providing this. Blank copies of the matrix form can be distributed, and as the possible solutions and criteria are generated, each participant can fill them in. Another method is to complete the lists of solutions and criteria, have them entered on a laptop computer, and print the matrix during a break. The three steps of listing solutions, setting criteria, and ranking the possibilities may even occur on three different occasions.

TIPS FOR FACILITATORS

Engage the group in a review of what was learned in answer to the "Where are we now?" and "Where do we want to go?" questions. Summarize what has been learned by study groups who have researched best practice to achieve the desired results.

Divide the large group into smaller groups or table teams and have them list all the possible strategies that might be employed to accomplish the goal or address the concern they have identified. As with brainstorming, encourage participants to generate as many variations and solutions as they can. Allow brief periods of wait time to stimulate more divergent thinking. Save the lists from all groups.

After a break or at another session within a few days, have the groups shift into a more reflective mode. Review the mission or belief statements that identify their core values. Ask them to consider what criteria would describe an ideal solution. List these criteria.

The decision matrix is constructed by listing the suggested changes or strategies along the left side of a grid. The criteria for a good decision become headings across the top.

To use the matrix, have participants go down each column and give each suggested solution a rating from 1 to 5, with 5 representing those suggestions that most closely fit the criteria heading for that column. Repeat this with each column. Participants can add the ratings across each row to get a total value for each of the suggested strategies. Their individual ratings can then be used in a whole group exercise, such as nominal group process or weighted voting.

FOR EXAMPLE

The elementary school team had reviewed test data and determined that one area of focus should be on improving reading achievement. Deciding how to accomplish this goal awoke a history of conflict between the "phonicians" and the "whole languagers." The progress that had been made to heal wounds and strengthen the school culture was at risk because the staff were approaching the goal of improved reading achievement as an either/or proposition. In fact, the facilitator had difficulty getting more than those two possible solutions generated in the first attempt at this process and had to temporarily abandon it.

Instead, the group put solutions on hold and began to generate criteria that would characterize a good solution. The members settled on the following:

- Would be consistent with our mission and beliefs
- Would help staff work together, not be divided
- Would include a component of parent participation
- Could be implemented with existing resources

As they focused on these criteria, they began to realize that neither phonics nor whole language, in and of themselves, would contain all of these elements. More ideas emerged for the "possible solutions" list, and they were able to construct their decision matrix. They realized that they had rejected a third program (Success for All) because they lacked the resources for full implementation of this labor-intensive approach. At the same time, they discovered that there were aspects of the model that they could adapt to their situation. What resulted was a unique approach that alternated days between whole language activities and cross-grade flexible skill grouping similar to the Joplin plan (which was one of the foundations of the Success for All design). They also discovered that parent volunteers could be readily engaged in whole-language-type activities, freeing teachers for more intense skill work with students. By focusing on their criteria, they invented their own creative solutions that, in turn, created a stronger sense of team.

A VARIATION

Another school was challenged by increasing enrollment and the district's decision to remedy overcrowding through the use of portable classrooms. Initial discussions about who or what should be housed in the portable classrooms were rapidly becoming characterized by discussions of seniority and comments like "I've taught in this room for 22 years and I only have 3 more to go and you'd have to carry me out in a coffin before I'd give up my room." As each grade level was listed for potential location in the portables, the objections changed from "They're too small to be wandering from one building to another; they might get lost" to "They're too big to be wandering from one building to another; they'll disrupt everything." The list of possible solutions then shifted to "special" programs. They were all written down, in spite of objections like "How can you have art without a sink?" and "Why have the traffic of all 500+ kids going back and forth when there's only a need for three or four classrooms?" and "You can't put the computer lab there because it would be too easy to break into."

Although the facilitator ignored the comments and objections when recording all the possible solutions, he reintroduced them during the discussion of criteria for a good decision. "I understand that security from break-ins is important. Do you want that as a criterion?" It was included, along with others like "least number of students moving" and "should fit program needs." As the criteria were identified, a whole new solution was introduced. Two teachers had wanted to try team teaching, but their rooms were too far apart and they had been afraid of the noise and hall traffic exchanging students. This suggestion started a whole new line of thought, and two primary teachers mentioned that they had been interested in multiage classrooms but hadn't thought too much about it because they were so crowded. The resulting decision was to use one portable for team teaching and one as a multiaged primary unit. Not only did the school solve its "who gets the portables?" problem, it had an opportunity to introduce two new instructional settings that had never been tried before because the interested teachers had been "locked into" their existing spaces.

Action Planning

A common characteristic of school improvement plans that never happen is that they identify strategies they will use (cooperative learning, a self-esteem program, multiple intelligences) without analyzing what implementation of those strategies will entail. Any one of the strategies mentioned represents many substeps needed to provide training and support for implementation. When schools identify popular topics like multiple intelligences and learning styles, their plans often involve training in the content knowledge without sufficient consideration of changes that would need to be made in the school itself to reflect those concepts. Although plans will surely be adjusted during implementation, they must be sufficiently developed to clearly represent the magnitude of change they require and the demands they will place on people, time, and budgets.

Purpose. An action plan is developed to lay out the specific steps that will be required to put a new strategy or program into place. Answering the question "How will we get there?" identified some "whats" (the strategies). Answering the "Where do we want to go?" question included focus on the belief system of the organization as "why." Action planning helps a group work out the who, when, where, and how.

When to use. Develop an action plan after the organization has set priorities for improvement, studied practices and programs that have been effective, and chosen the approaches best suited to their goals and school context.

Whom to involve. Because an action plan needs to identify specific steps, timelines, and resources, it is important to involve people who have information about and access to the school calendar and budget and who have a "big picture" perspective of all that is occurring in the organization. School teams often find it helpful to include a central office support person in the action-planning stage. If a major innovation such as multiage classrooms is being implemented, it is advisable to invite a consultant or a team member from another school that is already using the approach. These resource people can provide advice on how they approached the change and even more valuable insights about problems they didn't anticipate and what they might have done to avoid them.

The specificity required in action planning often brings the realization that the strategy or approach to be used is a much more complex change than it first appeared. In some situations, it is helpful to identify major subtasks and assign a small group to develop that part of the action plan. For example, a major change like multiage classrooms would need a component of parent education and communication. Involvement of parents in this planning subgroup would be essential.

Materials needed. Chart paper, markers, and large stick-on notes are commonly used for drafting an action plan as a group. It can then be typed into a laptop computer and printed for everyone to review. Once it is in the computer, it can readily be revised as it is adjusted throughout implementation.

TIPS FOR FACILITATORS

Formats for school improvement plans can be found in many of the resources listed in the annotated bibliography. Some action plans are developed in chart form, and others are written in narrative form. The common elements are steps to be taken, who will be involved, who will be responsible, resources needed, time required and schedule, and indicators of completion or progress. A simple way to begin is by using these elements as column headings on a large bulletin board or wall. The sequence of development is "work all the way down, and then across." In other words, first list all the steps that need to be taken. The facilitator will repeatedly ask "And what else does that involve?" This helps the group break down major tasks into their component parts. Another common question will be "What would need to happen before that?" This question guides the group to identify missing steps and create a sequence.

The group will continually recognize missing steps and rearrange the sequence of tasks, which can make very messy recording for the facilitator. Writing each task on a large stick-on note makes moving them around and inserting new ones neat and easy.

When the sequence of steps or tasks seems complete, the group works across the chart horizontally for each step. Identify the person responsible for each step and the people who will participate. Discuss whether there is a budgetary consideration. As they move to the timeline column, remind them that "time is money." If released time is going to be provided, there will be substitute costs. If compensation for time must be provided, that cost needs to be estimated. Timelines should consider the school calendar and capitalize on any staff development days or inservice time to fit with the school's action plan for improvement.

A most neglected but essential column is the last column, often given the heading of monitoring or evaluation. Too often, this column is simply used to check off completion of the activity, for example, "all staff attended a workshop on cooperative learning." This is inadequate because it does not assess whether anyone actually went back to his or her classroom and applied the knowledge and skills that were learned in the workshop. The example of brainstorming used in chapter 4 generated observable indicators that distinguish the behavior of lifelong learners. The criteria that will be observed or measured must be identified at the time the action plan is developed to ensure that progress can be reported in terms of results achieved, not just steps taken.

FOR EXAMPLE

Earlier in this chapter the group process technique of cause-and-effect (fishbone) diagramming was introduced with the example of a school leadership team that changed from revising an attendance policy to creating one-to-one mentor relationships between chronic absentees and caring adults in the school environment. Figure 5.3 shows the action plan the team developed to implement that new approach.

School: Anytown Middle School School Year(s): 1995-96

Improvement Objective: To improve student attendance

Members of Team or Task Force:

M. Black   M. Green
J. White   J. Jackson
B. Brown

Strategy: Develop 1:1 student-adult mentor
relationships for chronic absentees

Rationale: Research findings indicate that student engagement and personal bonding with adults in the school
are related to attendance and achievement

Activities: Steps to Be Taken	Persons Responsible	Persons Involved	Resources Needed	Timeline	Monitoring, Evaluation
Develop criteria to identify the chronic absentees	Counselors	SIT Subcommittee	Part of June workshop time	During June workshop	Criteria approved by SIT at August meeting
List the students who need to be involved	Counselor on SIT	Homeroom teachers	—	During June workshop	Presented and approved by SIT at August meeting

Figure 5.3. Action Plan for Mentor Program

Activity	Person responsible	Others involved	Materials	Timeline	Product
Set expectations for students who participate	Counselor on SIT	Homeroom teachers	—	During June workshop	Presented and approved by SIT at August meeting
Notify parents and get permission to contact students	Counselor	Counseling secretary	—	Before registration in August	Parent permissions returned
Set expectations for adult mentors	SIT subcommittee chair	SIT subcommittee	—	During June workshop	Approval by SIT at August meeting
Develop training for mentors	Assistant principal/staff development coordinator	SIT subcommittee/ homeroom teachers	Food for picnic	July	Approval by SIT at August meeting
Recruit and select mentors	Assistant principal	Homeroom teachers	—	July and August	List of mentors
Match students to mentors	Assistant principal	Counselors	—	July and August	List of possible matches

(continued)

Activities: Steps to Be Taken	Persons Responsible	Persons Involved	Resources Needed	Timeline	Monitoring, Evaluation
Hold mentor training and gain commitment	Assistant principal/staff development coordinator	Mentors/homeroom teachers	Stipends for 2-hour training sessions ($1,250) (25 mentors @ $50)	August	Mentors sign commitment forms
Hold meeting of students and mentors or make individual contact with students	Counselors/ assistant principal	Students/mentors/ homeroom teachers	—	August	Students return commitment forms
Determine times and places that mentors will contact students	Mentors	Students	—	First week of school	Schedules turned in to assistant principal

(continued)

Figure 5.3.

Schedule and hold mentor meetings	Assistant principal	Counselors/ mentors/homeroom teachers	Early release time once per month	Monthly, October–May	Minutes of meetings/summary of student attendance and grades
Reexamine attendance data	Counselors	—	—	Weekly by student; monthly for all	Graph attendance and grades each month as run charts
Plan celebration for mentors and students	Assistant principal	Students/mentors/ families/homeroom teachers	Budget for food, certificates, etc.	May	Progress certificates to students with % improvement

Figure 5.3. Continued

6

Answering the "How Will We Know We Are (Getting) There?" Question

It seemed like all my friends were going to exotic places that year. One group went to the Caribbean on spring break. Others were taking summer vacations in Europe. And a couple were going through the selection process for overseas teaching with the Department of Defense. All of them had invited me to come along, but I couldn't seem to muster much enthusiasm. Some recalcitrant part of me kept saying, "There are so many wonderful things to see in our own country. When I've done all the states, I'll start in on the world."

That made me curious about how many states I had already visited and which ones I would still need to see. On impulse, I bought a child's cardboard puzzle with each state outline forming a piece, and I glued on all the ones I'd been to as a child on family vacations or as an adult. I was amazed to discover that there were only 17 left, and most of them were in the Northeast. So while my friends planned for Europe, I planned for New England. I didn't want to be locked in with too tight a schedule to explore, but I did want my route laid out, so I had AAA prepare a Triptik for me. A Triptik is a set of maps about the size of a shopping list pad that's bound at the top with a coil. It's easy to hold and read while driving. Each page represents somewhere between 100 and 200 miles. For 3 1/2 weeks, I marked my progress by the number of pages flipped in my Triptik. When I got home, I celebrated my accomplishments by gluing 13 more state pieces onto my puzzle.

The journey of school improvement is much like that. An organization rarely reaches a state of completion as visible as the completed map of the United States. There will always be more destinations to pursue. Motivation has to come from proof of progress, because perfection will never be attained.

In previous chapters, we explored three of the critical questions of school improvement. The first was "Where are we now?" and required us to look carefully at the culture of our organization and at the performance of our students. Use of data was important in that answer. The second question was "Where do we want to go?" To set a clear goal, it was important to define the characteristics or observable indicators of the desired state in contrast to the status quo. The third question was "How will we get there?" and development of action plans required us to identify behaviors and results that can be observed or measured to demonstrate our progress.

If those first three phases were completed carefully, answering the question "How will we know we are getting there?" will be easy. That is why this chapter is fairly short and introduces few new tools. Knowing whether we are getting there simply means doing what we said we would do in our plan and checking what we said we would check. That is like the *D* (do) and the *C* (check) of the PDCA quality improvement cycle. In the RPTIM model, it is the *I* and the *M*. Wood used the *I* for implementation and the *M* to stand for maintenance. I believe *M* also must stand for monitoring. In the *Three Is* model, monitoring progress is the aspect of implementation without which institutionalization will never occur. No new practice can become part of "how we do things around here" until it has first moved from training to actual use. Three aspects of monitoring progress generate three additional questions:

- Are we reaching our goals?
- Are we coping with change?
- Are we fulfilling our mission?

Are We Reaching Our Goals?

In an earlier stage of school improvement, data were gathered on student achievement to assess the current situation. The same data should be compiled annually to develop a longitudinal look at progress, and the data can be portrayed in run charts.

When schools worked to identify "where we want to go," part of the effort was to take the major components of mission and belief statements and make them concrete with observable indicators. Gathering information on these indicators becomes part of the monitoring stage as schools answer the question "How will we know we are getting there?" The tools that were introduced to display data in chapters 3 and 4 are tools that will be used again and again throughout the process.

Many of us who learned and use Madeline Hunter's synthesis of research related to effective instruction have difficulty saying the word *monitor* without adding *and adjust.* This is very true for the implementation phase of school improvement. Although we needed specific action plans to set realistic timelines, acquire needed resources, and avoid overloading ourselves with too many complex efforts, those action plans must be considered "carved in Jell-O." If results cannot be observed, or changes are not those desired, school leadership teams must acknowledge and address those facts. They will need to identify whether the action plan is being implemented as intended, and they may have to modify it based on resources, unexpected barriers, and other needs that arise. Or they may need to reexamine whether the strategies selected for implementation need to be changed. However, school leaders must also use caution and guard against premature decisions to abandon a course before it has had time for a true test. The challenge is to strike a proper balance between flexibility and evolutionary planning on the one hand, and patience and perseverance on the other.

Monitoring progress is not always a sophisticated and complicated endeavor. When principals agree to conduct business on the roof or kiss a pig or sit in a dunking booth if students read a million pages—and parent volunteers construct a huge paper thermometer to count the pages read—that is monitoring of progress that can motivate continued effort until the real results (higher reading scores) can be documented.

FOR EXAMPLE

Their mission statement included the phrase "prepared to live in a democratic, pluralistic society." It sounded great. But the staff was concerned about the reality of the rhetoric. Their student population was quite homogeneous racially and economically, and they really wondered if students were aware of issues and needs outside their own environment. The observable behaviors that they decided to monitor were participation in student government, increased roles for students in shared decision making, active participation in that year's county and state elections, and participation in community service projects. Students in civics classes became involved in identifying opportunities for student involvement, and students in higher math classes gathered the information about participation.

Are We Coping With Change?

Organizations are made up of human beings with vast amounts of prior experience and a wide range of personal needs and interests. Knowing whether we are "getting there" must also consider these factors.

Children learn in different ways and at different speeds. In much the same way, adults adjust to change in different ways and at different rates. The concerns-based adoption model (CBAM) is based on studies of how teachers react to new innovations. One component of the model identifies a developmental sequence of stages of concern through which people move as they accept and adjust to change. *Taking Charge of Change*, published by the Association for Supervision and Curriculum Development, describes the progression of concerns:

- Awareness
- Information
- Personal
- Management
- Consequence
- Collaboration
- Refocusing

Once individuals in the organization become aware of an impending or developing change, their first concerns revolve around wanting to know more about it and how they will be affected personally. As their questions are answered and they become willing to attempt the new practice, their concerns relate to how they will manage logistics such as time, materials, and record keeping. When these concerns of self and the task are addressed, teachers become more interested in how their use of a new practice is affecting students. More advanced stages of concern relate to sharing their new efforts with colleagues and using their own ideas to modify and improve the new practice. As part of CBAM, the researchers developed procedures for assessing the concerns of individuals within the organization.

Stages of Concern Questionnaire

The Stages of Concern Questionnaire (SoCQ) is a survey instrument that includes 35 items and requires only 10-15 minutes to administer. It can be hand or machine scored. The result is a profile that shows the intensity of each concern for that respondent. Average scores of groups or subgroups can be calculated.

Purpose. The SoCQ and the variations described below are designed to identify the most intense concerns being felt by individuals and groups in the organization. This information is valuable in planning organizational responses and support for its members.

When to use. The formal SoCQ procedure is generally used when research or program evaluation is being conducted. It can also be used to provide diagnostic information during the course of a change process. It can be administered several times during the course of a year without losing its reliability.

Whom to involve. The SoCQ can be used with an entire school or district population in its machine-scorable form.

Materials needed. The survey items and quick-scoring device are included in *Taking Charge of Change*. Respondents will need the survey form and pencils. For large groups, answer sheets that can be scanned and analyzed should be used.

TIPS FOR FACILITATORS

The SoCQ itself is easy to administer, and the profiles produced from the results appear deceptively self-evident. The challenge is to interpret them accurately and respond appropriately. Study the descriptions in *Taking Charge of Change* carefully. If the SoCQ is to be used for formal program evaluation, the SoCQ manual and training in interpretation of SoCQ profiles should be acquired.

FOR EXAMPLE

In the Winter 1995 issue of the *Journal of Staff Development*, Stephen Anderson, Carol Rolheiser, and Barrie Bennett report their use of the SoCQ to document the experiences of teachers who were implementing cooperative learning. They discovered that the teachers surveyed seemed to cluster into three groups, which they called nonusers, tentative beginning users, and experienced beginning users. They identified nine concerns that were common to all three groups, although they varied in intensity from group to group:

- Impact on teaching strategies
- Curriculum integration
- Time for implementation
- Student participation
- Individualization
- Student assessment and evaluation
- Student outcomes
- Collaboration with other teachers
- Quality of implementation

Because these concerns were felt by all participants, the authors were able to suggest alterations in the schools' staff development programs that would respond and provide support for growth to the next stage.

A VARIATION

The SoCQ is the most formal method of identifying the concerns felt by participants in a change process. *Taking Charge of Change* also describes the use of face-to-face conversations in which the facilitator asks very simple questions like "How do you feel about _____ ?" and may follow up with more specific probes. This informal dialogue has been referred to as a "one-legged interview" because it should be concise enough to be completed before the facilitator would lose her balance if she were on one leg. To interpret the responses correctly, the facilitator must not interrupt and then must reflect on the entire conversation and analyze it holistically to assess the stage of concern being expressed.

ANOTHER TWIST

The authors of *Taking Charge of Change* also describe the use of an open-ended statement like "When you think about _____, what are your concerns?" Their recommendations are to regard this as more formal than the face-to-face conversation, encouraging respondents to answer in complete sentences. They also suggest two forms of analysis, first considering each sentence separately and then rereading and analyzing the tone of the whole response.

To use the open-ended statement for program evaluation or research, facilitators should read the authors' recommendations carefully and be very thorough in their interpretation. I have found that a very informal open-ended statement can provide valuable information for purposes of "quick and dirty" diagnosis and adjustments to staff development activities. I include an item like "My biggest concern about _____ at this time is _____" on feedback forms at the end of training sessions. Although the interpretation can hardly be called scientific, I review the feedback forms with stages of concern in mind, and this helps me make adjustments in follow-up sessions. It also indicates whether participants share common concerns or have a wide range of needs that will require a greater variety of responses.

Are We Fulfilling Our Mission?

The importance of gathering and using data at all stages of the improvement process was emphasized in response to the question "Are we reaching our goals?" In the same way, articulating the values and beliefs of the organization must be a part of every phase of change. Developing a mission *statement* may be an activity. Developing a *sense* of mission is an ongoing process. While focusing on documented results in student achievement, for example, school leaders must not forget to monitor the norms and values of the school culture.

One school was well known for its many ways of recognizing positive student behavior. "Catch them being good" was a favorite saying, and one method the staff used was to make a quick note of something positive done or said by a student and place the slip of paper in a suggestion-box-type container in the office. Each time the announcements were given, the principal would draw a few items at random from the box and read them. As the school leadership team thought about maintaining focus on the mission and on belief statements, team members decided to modify the process slightly and include both students and adults. "Catch them being good" became "notice people doing things that exemplify our mission." The principal's reporting of mission-oriented actions created much greater interest and meaning than mere recitation of the mission statement.

Chapter 3 was about knowing where we are now. Chapter 4 emphasized deciding where we want to go. Chapter 5 addressed decisions about how to get there. The message of chapter 6 has been like the Nike commercial—Just do it®—and courageously check to be sure it's working.

7

Answering the
"How Will We Sustain the
Focus and Momentum?"
Question

N ot long ago, I watched the city of Baltimore honor a hero. Cal Ripken, Jr. had broken Lou Gehrig's record of playing in 2,130 consecutive games. The numerals on the warehouse across from the diamond flipped to 2,131 and the crowd went wild. Cal just smiled and loped around the field like he wasn't too sure what the fuss was all about. How did he reach that milestone? He just kept showing up for work. Along the way, he struck out at the plate now and then and recorded some errors in his position as shortstop. But he just kept showing up for work and doing his best. He knew how to sustain focus and momentum.

How can travelers on the road to school improvement develop that same tenacity? How do school leaders add momentum to the M of maintenance in RPTIM? How does the innovation that was implemented in response to "How will we get there?" become institutionalized so it is taken for granted as "just the way we do things around here"? Quality improvement users would say that you do so by repeating the PDCA cycle—now that you've checked what you've done, act on the information, and start again with planning. Those steps are important, but inadequate. They overestimate the power of technical processes and underestimate the power of the prevailing school culture. The scientific law that an object at rest tends to remain at rest is nowhere more true than in traditional organizations. Great leaders and great ideas have sparked new efforts that blaze briefly and sputter into oblivion because they are smothered under the overwhelming weight of the school culture. Lasting change requires reculturing, reshaping the norms of the organization—what the 1980s gurus called paradigm shifting. This chapter describes five actions that are needed to sustain change:

- Continue training and coaching
- Cope with conflict
- Engage in sustained inquiry
- Refocus and reaffirm organizational values
- Support leaders and followers

Continue Training and Coaching

A difficulty with every school improvement project I have encountered is that the schools spend too large a proportion of their professional development resources on training before implementing a new innovation. The implication is that we can "front-end load" a process that takes years and requires individual movement through several stages of acceptance and use. The assumption is that adult learners can acquire new skills all at once, in isolation from practice, and can retain and retrieve them for use once the system has removed barriers and set them free to proceed. Conducting all the training at the beginning further ignores the reality that over a period of years, there is staff turnover. New people join the organization who were never introduced to techniques they will be expected to use. The quality management concept of "just in time" training is not a panacea but does respond to the adult learners' need for job relevancy and immediate application of the new learning.

Continued training should be of two types. Introductory or basic training should be repeated on a cyclical basis to include new staff members and those who may have attended earlier training but not had a chance to implement it yet. For instructional approaches as complex as cooperative learning, interdisciplinary teaching, or learning styles, a sequence from basic to more advanced training experiences should be provided. These levels of training can respond to the needs of participants as they move through the stages of concern. Knowing that a higher level of training is available can also stimulate the progress of more cautious adopters.

Coaching is different from training and resembles the guided-practice stage of instruction. Feedback is needed for those who are most active with the new technique, as well as those who are least skilled. The leaders need to refine and polish their practice, because they are models for others and need to be sure they are providing accurate examples. Those least skilled, or most reluctant, need coaching to convey the expectation that they will continue to improve their art and craft in line with organizational goals.

Cope With Conflict

It is in the nature of humans to differ, and from those differences conflicts are bound to arise. One of the most popular topics for consultants in the 1990s is conflict resolution. Unfortunately, the term *resolution* implies an unrealistic expectation that conflict can be eliminated and that the presence of conflict is a bad thing. I prefer to talk about managing conflict or coping with conflict because it acknowledges that a certain amount is unavoidable and that, in fact, productive organizations often encourage it. Dynamic organizations are not populated by clones. "Groupthink" is a powerful killer of creativity. There are four techniques that I have used successfully to cope with conflict: Venn diagrams, Quick-Writes, TalkWalks, and Go for the Green.

Venn Diagrams

A Venn diagram is simply a set of two or more circles. They are drawn to intersect, be concentric, or not touch at all as a way of illustrating relationships. The name comes from their originator, mathematician John Venn, who specialized in logic.

Purpose. A Venn diagram can be used to illustrate complex relationships, display data, or generate discussion for problem solving and decision making. Venn diagrams help groups compare and contrast multiple sets of ideas or interests and are particularly valuable for demonstrating relationships that are difficult to describe in words.

When to use. When members of a group are polarized and lack a sense of common ground, a Venn diagram can reopen communication and refocus the group.

Whom to involve. All members of the group, or parties to a conflict, should contribute to the Venn diagram.

Materials needed. Paper and pencil are sufficient. Chart paper and stick-on notes are useful for constructing Venn diagrams that can be seen and discussed by larger groups.

TIPS FOR FACILITATORS

Describe the purpose of a Venn diagram and present a simple example. Engage the group in determining how many circles will be needed and predicting how much they will overlap. Give instructions about writing their responses, one on each stick-on note. Small groups may sketch their own Venn diagram to share, or a large diagram can be developed as participants post their stick-on notes. Be flexible and add or move circles as the group's responses are compiled.

FOR EXAMPLE

To answer the "Where do we want to go?" question, a Venn diagram can be used to discover the common values and beliefs held by various stakeholder groups. Each group (parents, teachers, community members, students) can meet separately and write its beliefs or interests, one per stick-on note. A large Venn diagram can be drawn with a circle representing each of the groups. The stick-on notes can then be placed in separate or overlapping areas of the circles. This communicates visually which values are shared by which groups. If even a few stick-on notes land in the centermost overlapping area, the group can see that there are shared values on which to build.

In many districts, the public is calling for renewed emphasis on character education but have very diverse agendas as to what should be included. Some school leaders have courageously brought conflicting groups together to seek common ground. Figure 7.1 is a Venn diagram that illustrates the consensus reached.

VARIATIONS

Venn diagrams can be used during almost any phase of an improvement process. To answer the "Where are we now?" question, a

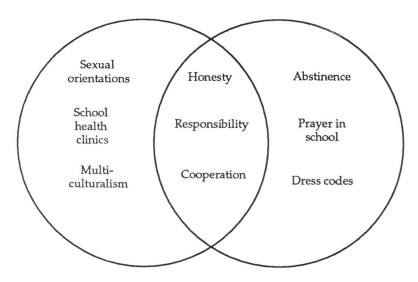

Figure 7.1. Venn Diagram of Topics for Character Education

group could use the circles to represent major forces or entities in the organization and how they are related or influence each other.

Quick-Writes

A Quick-Write is similar to the informal stream-of-consciousness writing that is done in keeping a journal or log. A prompt is given and participants are encouraged to record their thoughts as they emerge.

Purpose. The purpose of a Quick-Write is to provide an opportunity for individual, reflective thinking about the topic or issue at hand.

When to use. Quick-Write can be used before initiating discussion about a complex or controversial issue. In this case, the purpose is to help participants clarify their own viewpoints and prepare words with which to express themselves before launching into position statements. Quick-Write is also helpful as a tension reliever if a serious discussion is deadlocked or is becoming too inflammatory. Participants are asked to take a silent break and put their current position or issues into writing. This guides them to refocus and then reopen the discussion on a more positive note.

Whom to involve. When Quick-Write is used to open discussion, or deal with conflicts, all parties should be involved.

Materials needed. Individual paper and writing instruments should be supplied. Markers and chart paper should not be in evidence because Quick-Write participants are promised confidentiality.

TIPS FOR FACILITATORS

Provide a writing prompt in the form of a sentence stem or heading. Assure participants that they are writing to clarify their own thoughts and decide how they can best express those thoughts to others. Their writing remains their own property and they only share what they decide to after they have completed the activity.

FOR EXAMPLE

The district's Site-Based Management Advisory Committee was meeting in an attempt to create better understanding between principals and representatives from some schools who felt that they were not being given enough authority in enough areas of school operation. Some of the parents and community members had complained to board members that principals were "holding out" and trying to retain control. Principals were upset and feeling threatened. Among themselves and to a few district administrators, they whispered that the district was "giving the ship away" and that it seemed unfair for them to be held accountable for their school's success when the decisions were being taken out of their hands.

As an outside facilitator, I began the meeting by asking participants to do some writing on a form I had prepared. The blue sheets that I gave to principals had these headings:

I became a principal because I wanted to:	Even though I knew I would have to:

The green sheets given to parent and community representatives were headed:

I want to be part of these decisions:	But not deal with these decisions:

When the participants had received their sheets, I asked them how much work time they would need, and I emphasized that they would be working independently. A time limit of 5 minutes was set and they began to write.

When the time period was up, I asked them to form groups with 2-3 blue sheets and 2-3 green sheets in evidence. Their instructions were to share their thoughts with each other. They could simply place their sheets on the table next to each other and make comparisons, or set their sheets aside and just express the overall feelings that emerged as they reflected on their roles in shared decision making.

Some groups looked at each other warily and communication was slow to start. Other groups were able to very candidly compare their feelings. They discovered that principals had worked hard to achieve administrative roles because they wanted to be instructional leaders. They wanted to work with teachers to improve instruction and wanted to be advocates for children. These were their primary motivators, in spite of their knowledge that they would have to deal with personnel issues and budget management and paperwork for the organization. Parent and community members had indicated that they wanted to talk about what should be in the curriculum and how teachers should teach—maybe even evaluate teachers, but not be involved in firing them or in dealing with any element of "the bureaucracy." As they talked, the site-based management team members began to realize that they had been pushing to take over all the things that principals had seen as their real purpose and leave principals with only those tasks that were "the drudgery." Some principals began quietly to share how it felt to work for years trying to develop leadership skills and feel reduced to being a manager of the noneducational aspects of the school. This open discussion was the first step toward defining the roles of stakeholder groups and clarifying the scope of site-based management for the district.

TalkWalks

TalkWalking is a technique I learned from my friend Pam Robbins, who developed it in collaboration with a physician friend. It is based on the practice of "going on rounds" with students and colleagues in a teaching hospital. It adds the kinesthetic learning modality to what are often "sit and get" experiences.

Purpose. Going on a TalkWalk provides an opportunity for colleagues to exchange viewpoints in an informal atmosphere. It combines interaction with the stimulation of exercise and a change of scenery. The movement and change of environment are helpful in overcoming inhibitions and promoting a sense of well-being.

When to use. A TalkWalk can be helpful on many occasions. It can be used toward the end of a workshop to allow participants to discuss the implications of what they have learned and how they can apply it in their job role. It can also become an informal part of the school culture. Staff members can choose times to meet for both mental and physical exercise, combining a brisk walk with discussion of an article they have read or an idea they would like to try. Colleagues can use a TalkWalk to seek each other's advice on a challenge they are currently facing. As a tool for coping with conflict, a TalkWalk can provide a chance to ease a group out of a tense situation or nonproductive discussion by breaking them into smaller groups and moving them into another setting.

Whom to involve. Any group of two or three people can engage in a TalkWalk. In addition to workshop participants, variations have included teachers and students, or principal and teacher(s). One friend of mine declares that a TalkWalk is the only way she's ever found to get her teenage son to open up and communicate with her.

Materials needed. The ideal environment for TalkWalking is a place where participants can actually get outdoors and walk around the block or parking lot. TalkWalking has also been effective in the confines of hotel corridors and conference centers. The main requirement is space to move out and away from the confines of the existing situation—both mentally and physically.

Set a time limit and a topic. Create a definite expectation that this is not just "an extra break" but a task-oriented activity time. State the purpose clearly, such as "come back with your analysis of why we are having difficulty with this topic and your recommendation of where we should go from here."

Use your own discretion about forming the dyads or trios for TalkWalking. On some occasions, I have orchestrated the structure to get particular participants or groups talking to each other or to break up certain combinations that are sidetracking the whole group. Unless there is a specific reason for directing the structure of the groups, voluntary choices of partners are best.

FOR EXAMPLE

It was a long, hot summer. I was one of several consultants hired to provide training for school leadership teams who would face new responsibilities under new state legislation. Two week-long institutes had already been held, with good results. The in-state facilitators who were working with me had done a great job, the content was well received, and the groups had left with the first draft of a school improvement plan in hand so they could complete it at their schools and submit it to the state in a timely manner. This Monday morning was totally unlike the others. When the state facilitators and I arrived, the people at the host school were very friendly, but had no knowledge about the supplies and materials we were expecting. Coffeepots had been packed away for the summer, and their whereabouts was unknown—always a bad sign. The participants arrived and were polite, but they seemed very distant and wary. As I began the overview of the week and talked about the final product we would create by Friday, they became more tense. The body language became rigid and hostile, and it was almost impossible to establish eye contact.

After struggling for nearly an hour, I decided to stop talking and introduce a short videotape. While I "huddled" with my copresenters to analyze the situation, I watched them pass written notes and exchange nonverbal messages that seemed less than positive. My colleagues couldn't shed any light on what was happening, so I decided to take a risk and confront the situation. It didn't seem like I had a lot to lose, because I'd never had them with me anyway.

When the videotape was over, I told them that I'd like to give them a chance to discuss the ideas in it, but that I also needed their help. I described the feeling I had that we were not quite on the same wavelength and that I'd appreciate their suggestions on what might be done to create a better climate. I then described a TalkWalk and asked them to come back in 10 minutes. By then, coffee would be ready and we would take a 15-minute break (emphasizing that the walk was an activity, not a break). I asked them to either have the bravest member of their group talk to me during the break, or give me an anonymous written note of feedback.

I wasn't sure how to interpret the enthusiasm with which they accepted the opportunity to get together and move out, but they did accept the assignment. The feedback I received was invaluable. They had been shocked at my opening comments that they were members of leadership teams and that we would be working together on improvement plans for their school. Many of them had been contacted just the week before and had been asked to attend a 5-day workshop. They were going to receive a stipend for attending, with an option of graduate credit, and the only prerequisite they knew about was that they were available. I asked them to set aside their confusion about their roles and learn what they could that day about the research on effective schools while I sought clarification of their responsibilities.

That evening was spent on the telephone. Many calls flew back and forth to and from staff members at the state education department, local district administrators, my copresenters, and me. We asked administrators from each district to come the next morning and meet with their participants to clarify the purpose of the workshop, and their responsibilities that week and in follow-up with their schools. To their credit, every district cooperated, and the first part of Tuesday morning was spent in break-out rooms laying the groundwork that should have been in place earlier. Some people dropped out and left. Those who stayed became one of the most cooperative groups I've worked with, eager to learn and fulfill their roles.

That TalkWalk provided the tension release they needed and the information I needed on which to make changes in our relationship and purpose. I hate to speculate on what would have happened without it.

Go for the Green

Bob Garmston introduced this activity at a workshop called Premier Presentation Skills, which I attended several years ago. It is one of the most valuable techniques I have found to address conflicts and nonproductive behavior in groups.

Purpose. Go for the Green appeals to the senses through its use of color and metaphor. The purpose is to identify possible causes for nonproductive behavior and shift the focus from the problem behavior or the problem people to factors that can be changed more readily.

When to use. Go for the Green can be used when a group, or the facilitators of a group, are aware of a behavior pattern that is interfering with its effectiveness.

Whom to involve. The entire group can be involved if the problem has been identified by the group as a whole. If only the facilitators or a few group members have become concerned about a pattern or situation, they can use Go for the Green to analyze it and develop strategies for dealing with it.

Materials needed. To use Go for the Green, you will need large chart paper and black, green, and red markers.

TIPS FOR FACILITATORS

Start with a red circle in the middle of the chart paper. Let the group know that you are using that color deliberately, because there seems to be a situation that is "making them see red" or is "stopping" them from accomplishing their tasks. Involve the group in deciding on a label to designate the difficult behavior or situation. For example, the team described below was frustrated because team members continually engaged in side conversations and then didn't know what was going on in the discussion. Ideas had to be repeated for them and time was wasted.

When the problem has been identified in red, switch to the black marker and write across the top of the page "Under what conditions would I . . ." Ask participants to think about reasons they might exhibit that behavior themselves. While they are thinking, switch to the green marker. As they share their thoughts, record them in green on diagonal lines going out from the red circle, like rays on a child's drawing of the sun.

Once the possible causes have been recorded, urge the group to "go for the green" rather than rave about the red. Talk about the various causes and how they might be changed, or what accommodations could be made to decrease them.

Two aspects of this technique reduce conflict. By thinking about "why I might . . . ," critics who have complained usually realize that they've been guilty of the same behavior at some point. By going for the green, group members and facilitators often recognize ways in which their own planning (or lack of) has contributed to the difficulty.

FOR EXAMPLE

The leaders of the team were frustrated because it seemed like they could never get anything completed in the time available for team meetings. Certain combinations of team members would sit together and engage in side conversations throughout the meeting. When their attention would return to the discussion at hand, they would ask people to repeat their statements. If the chairperson asked, "Have we reached a decision?" they would emerge and need a summary of what had transpired and what the tentative conclusion was. They asked me for some idea of how to handle this problem, and I asked if they had a few minutes to learn a new group process technique. They were eager for a new tool, and I conducted a quick Go for the Green activity with them. Figure 7.2 shows the result.

They looked at it for a while and asked if this was what I thought they should do with the group. I said they might want to use it at some time but asked them to look at it again and see if it gave them any ideas of things they might try first. They ended up with a list of strategies that matched the possible causes:

- Changing the room configuration so everyone could be around the same table
- Guiding the "side conversers" to other seats by setting up name cards on tables before the meeting
- Allocating a few minutes at the start of the agenda for participants to "check in" and focus on the purpose of the meeting

Under what conditions might I engage in . . .

Figure 7.2. Go for the Green on Side Conversations

- Having a timekeeper monitor the agenda
- Calling on these participants for their viewpoints early in the discussion of each topic

The concerned participants decided to try these strategies first without confronting the behavior in the whole group. If that didn't work, they were going to call me and ask me to come and do Go for the Green and some other work on meeting behavior with their team. I haven't heard from them. I hope that means their strategies worked.

Engage in Sustained Inquiry

The rhetoric of the 1990s includes phrases like school of learners, learning community, lifelong learning, and collaborative inquiry. All of these indicate a need for educators to model the motivation and skills of continued study and professional growth. This book was designed around a set of questions to convey that school change occurs through ongoing cycles of inquiry: asking critical questions, seeking answers, proposing and testing solutions, and refining and renewing the process.

It is in the nature of books to start with a chapter 1 and end after some sequence of content has been presented. The process of change and improvement is not that linear. It is cyclical, but even more complex than a single cycle. At any given time, members of the organization may be engaged in study of several aspects of the school or district. A more accurate visual image of continuous improvement would be a corkscrew or Slinky toy, which consists of a series of spirals.

Action research as a technique of sustained inquiry is presented in this chapter to emphasize its importance in maintaining the momentum of change and improvement. Several writers on action research describe stages of problem analysis, data collection, data analysis, planning action programs, implementing them, and evaluating the results. By that definition, this entire book describes a process that is ongoing action research.

Action Research

Action research is a method of participatory involvement in both individual and group learning. It is one of the few techniques that bridges the individuality of traditional staff development and the common effort of school improvement and organizational development. Action research expands the definition of "teacher" from deliverer of content to scholar of the processes of teaching and learning and investigator of the context of schooling. Participants in action research become more reflective practitioners and are also in a most unique position to bridge the gap between K-12 and higher education.

Purpose. Action research is conducted for a number of specific reasons, but the overall purpose is to improve the teaching and learning process in the school. Because participants study topics, problems, or programs related to their roles and interests, it makes inservice more relevant. Collegial relationships are strengthened, and the likelihood that what participants learn will be accepted by others in the school is increased.

When to use. Action research is used constantly in a dynamic organization. Gathering data to better understand "Where are we now?" qualifies as action research to many writers. Investigating the possible causes of problems and concerns to decide "Where do we want to go?" and "How will we get there?" also qualifies as action research to some. Experts with the most rigorous definitions of action research would place it in the context of piloting a new approach or program and evaluating whether it is working as well as intended or better than other practices. Because this book is written for active practitioners looking at real problems in their schools in the most timely and practical ways, all those activities qualify as action research. However, such an open definition may not be acceptable to university partners in collaborative projects such as professional development schools and research and development centers.

Whom to involve. The literature on action research describes three forms: individual, collaborative, and schoolwide. This book outlines a schoolwide process guided by a leadership team, in which the scope of the study encompasses the school as a whole, incorporates stakeholder input, and develops action plans that affect all members of the organization. Individual action research can be conducted independently by teachers trying something new within their own classrooms. Collaborative action research involves members of the school staff working as peers. It may also include support and participation by district-level staff and university or college partners. Decisions about whom to involve will emerge when the action research question has been clearly stated and the audience for the findings has been identified.

Materials needed. Materials needed vary greatly based on the purpose of the action research. They may include literature to review, technical support to gather and analyze data, or additional instructional materials to use with new teaching strategies.

TIPS FOR FACILITATORS

One of the purposes and benefits of action research is to switch the ownership for change and improvement to the participants within the organization. To achieve this purpose, the role of the facilitator should be advisory and supportive, not central to the effort. As a "guide on the side," there are important ways a facilitator can assist.

First, ask probing questions to help the individual or group frame the research problem or question accurately and specifically. The statement "I want to see if cooperative learning really works" is a signal that such guidance is needed. Second, emphasize the need to gather appropriate data from which to draw conclusions. Third, discuss the purpose, methods, and data for the study to be sure they are congruent.

Also, identify needs for outside expertise and enlist support. For example, if an action research project will include quantitative data analysis, it may be important to include a district-level or university partner as consultant or team member. When deciding whether to pursue a university partnership, it is important to remember that a faculty member's reward system is based on conducting research that can be published. In many settings, professors are vulnerable if they spend too much time working with schools in a service capacity. No matter how dedicated they are to supporting the public schools, they will be most interested in projects that address general questions applicable to all schools, are grounded in a particular theory base, and involve rigorous use of data. If those are characteristics of your action research project, it would be wise to seek a higher education partnership. If your focus is primarily internal and pragmatic, expertise from the district or an intermediate service agency may be more appropriate.

Finally, consider the audience for the results of the project. If an individual teacher wants to see whether certain rewards he offers will increase the completion of homework assignments, that teacher is his only audience. If a teaching strategy or concept such as learning styles is being piloted by one group of teachers with the intent of testing it for possible schoolwide adoption, the audience is much wider and the considerations are more complex. As a facilitator or coach, help the project participants anticipate the questions that will be asked by other staff members and be sure that the project will address them.

FOR EXAMPLE

Teachers in a junior high school were concerned about poor attendance patterns of their students. They discussed possible reasons for poor attendance at length. About the same time, some of them had been reading about student engagement in learning. A few others had attended a workshop on cooperative learning. They felt that use of cooperative learning might increase achievement and might seem more engaging to the students. Social studies teachers decided to work together and develop cooperative learning activities. Their goal was to have a cooperative learning activity every Thursday and see what would happen.

The data-gathering aspect of their project was overlooked at the time but eventually became an "aha!" event for the entire school. After a month or so, the guidance counselor reported at a faculty meeting that for some reason, school attendance in seventh and eighth grade was showing an increase and was higher on Thursdays than any other day of the week. He wondered if anyone was doing anything special on Thursdays. When the social studies teachers mentioned their experiment, the language arts teachers decided to test it further. They chose Tuesday as a day to use cooperative learning and consciously set out to have the counselor help them trace the attendance patterns. At the time I lost contact with this school, they had not yet determined the effects, if any, on student achievement, but they had certainly made an impact on student interest and stimulated discussion throughout the school.

Refocus and Reaffirm Organizational Values

Growth, change, improvement—these are easy words, but hard work. Only our intrinsic values keep us dedicated to a cause that is difficult and unending. All of us have seen great programs come and go, not because they didn't have good results but because we got tired and returned to old ways that were not actually better—they were just easier.

In our personal lives, most of us would admit the tendency to get so caught up in the demands of our daily lives that we lose touch with our own values. In moments of stress, we hear ourselves say things or find ourselves doing things that are completely out of sync with our own ideals and beliefs. We discover we're driving just as rudely as everyone else in our city. We can't remember the last time we thought about our personal faith or the philosophy of education we brought to our work years ago. Or we realize we are not doing things—like "random acts of kindness"—that we do consider important and that we want our students, peers, and families to value. Sometimes we wonder how we got into such a state.

Just like individuals, organizations lose touch and lose their way when there is no time to reflect on the meaning of what we do each day. Dynamic organizations constantly reaffirm their organizational values and mission. Some ways to maintain this focus include reflective study groups; conscious decisions about abandoning, synthesizing, rejecting, or integrating current and new practices; and public celebration of organizational achievements.

Reflective Study Groups

The earlier discussion of action research has many features in common with this description of reflective study groups. In fact, people doing action research are sometimes called study groups, project teams, quality teams, or site councils. The more important word in this setting is *reflective*. These are small groups of people who want more from staff development than "getting something new I can use in class tomorrow." These are members of the organization who want to think about implications and concerns and consistency with goals. They are small groups who may meet over lunch once a week, for breakfast on the way to school, or in other environments they choose. They exist for a semester at a time, or they may go on and on. If they have not evolved in your school or district, they need to be initiated and nurtured because they are vital to the "soul" of the organization.

Purpose. Reflective study groups fulfill many purposes. They contribute to development of new knowledge bases within the school. They raise awareness of needs within the organization and provide feedback by pointing out discrepancies between practice and stated beliefs. Reflective study groups engage in a high level of professional dialogue that is similar to peer coaching. They study new literature and discuss its merits. They encourage each other to try new practices. Perhaps their most unique characteristic is that they challenge each other with probing questions about their experiences. What happened? How and why? What feelings were created? What possible alternatives could be proposed? What plans could we suggest for next time?

When to use. Reflective study groups can be formed and perform successfully when a climate of trust has been established between the participants and within the organization. Participants within the study group need to establish norms that anything may be questioned but that the questions are not judgmental and that specific conversations are confidential. Decisions about communicating information and feedback to the whole school are made jointly and phrased objectively before being passed along.

Whom to involve. A rule of thumb on appropriate size for reflective study groups is three to seven participants. At the beginning, members of the group should be individuals with some common interests and prior experience working together as a foundation for the trust level that is essential. Thinking or learning style is a factor to consider as well. With my apologies for this oversimplification, it appears that the concrete, linear thinkers do best or are most comfortable on action research teams with a specific design, whereas the more abstract thinkers contribute greatly to the process of reflection.

Materials needed. Reflective study groups often begin as ways for colleagues to share things they have read and learned and get reactions from each other. Multiple copies of articles or books may be needed for this purpose. As study groups begin to focus on practices within the school and compare them to the best practices and new developments they read about, they may need access to various kinds of data and assistance interpreting it. One of the most important resources they will need is access to the ears of leadership as they identify new ideas and areas for possible improvement within the school.

Tips for Facilitators

A key role of the facilitator is to establish the norms of respect and confidentiality within the study group. You may be asked to help the group identify a theme for its study, acquire and assemble materials, organize meeting times, record main points made by the group, and provide guidance about how to share the group's new knowledge and ideas with the rest of the staff. It would be unusual for all staff to look on the work of reflective study groups as relevant and irresistible, so prepare them for and help them deal with staff reactions and resistance.

FOR EXAMPLE

Years ago, some colleagues and I formed what I believe constitutes a reflective study group even though it did not emerge as a planned entity according to the suggestions given here. There just happened to be a bunch of us who belonged to the Association for Supervision and Curriculum Development and received the ASCD's journal *Educational Leadership* every month. One day, we were lamenting about how hard it was to keep up with our professional reading and to know how to share it with the rest of the school. This was before I knew anything about cooperative learning jigsaws, but we decided to divide up the table of contents each time, read our articles, and "sneak" over to McDonald's for lunch 1 day per week and talk about them. Others became curious about what we were doing and asked us to give them summaries of good information we found. Although we had no formal role, I believe we contributed to the learning of the organization.

VARIATIONS

Some study groups have tried to select excellent articles and make copies to put in everyone's mailbox, but they have been disappointed with the lack of reaction to them. Other groups have told me about two strategies that seem to work better. Rather than distributing the whole article, they prepare a very short summary on a 3" × 5" card that they distribute. They mention that the full article is posted in several key places in the school and invite anyone interested to talk to one of them about it or meet with them for breakfast on an appointed day.

Another school told me about how they post an article on a large piece of bulletin board paper in the lounge. They highlight the main points so it can be rapidly skimmed, and they hang markers beside it. Casual readers leave "graffiti" comments about the article, which prompt others to read and react as well. The informal reaction energizes the thinking of the staff and sometimes generates ideas for consideration that are brought to the school leadership team and then presented to the whole faculty.

Abandon, Synthesize, Reject, and Integrate

There is a grave danger in learning too much about too many new things. The danger is that we can't do them all and still maintain the degree of focus that is needed to move the whole organization forward together. The effective schools work of Ron Edmonds and Larry Lezotte used the phrase "organized abandonment" to describe a process of looking carefully at existing practices and discontinuing those that are neither effective nor consistent with the values of the organization.

Another way to keep the organization focused is to be sure that similar projects and programs are synthesized into a common effort. Especially at the district level, a function of organizational development is to "let the right hand know what the left hand is doing" and merge their efforts. For example, I once attended a principals' meeting where one of the curriculum specialists described a computer program he had set up to keep textbook inventory and how they should handle "loaning" textbooks from building to building so the inventory would remain accurate. The audience did not seem appreciative of his efforts. Later, I learned that there was already a software system for keeping track of textbooks that had been developed by the Media and Technology division. These two projects needed to be synthesized and simplified so principals could focus on their organization's core values of teaching and learning.

Celebrate

A major emphasis of chapter 6 was the importance of identifying indicators to monitor and gathering data to verify that an improvement plan is actually being implemented and is achieving the intended results. Those are technical aspects of change and accountability. In this chapter, the emphasis is sustaining change and improvement as part of the culture of the organization. The indicators and data are just as essential, but for a different purpose.

Most of us are comfortable with the phrase "nothing succeeds like success" and mentally apply it to teaching students at the appropriate level of difficulty so they will be successful and motivated to keep trying and make further progress. The same phrase and logic applies to organizational change. We can't keep on devoting energy above and beyond the call of duty without evidence that it is getting us somewhere. No school or district has the financial resources to provide extrinsic rewards commensurate with the amount of effort required to keep an organization focused on continuous improvement. We need evidence of progress to celebrate and rejuvenate our own energy.

Terry Deal was one of the first to transfer his work on corporate culture to the context of schools, and any of his writing will be helpful. The more recent work of Michael Fullan and Tom Sergiovanni refers to reculturing and the spiritual element of schools as organizations. When benchmarks are reached or milestones achieved, call on the staff members who love drama, the former cheerleaders, the social organizers, and plan unique ways to celebrate!

Support Leaders and Followers

Organizational change may be an oxymoron like jumbo shrimp. Organizations don't change as whole entities. They change as the people within them do, and those people don't change all at the same time. There are leaders, and there are optimistic followers, and there are pessimistic, reluctant followers, and there are some who don't budge at all. Those who lead the way—and those who readily join them—need support to weather initial resistance and continue their efforts. They need technical support to help get the actual work done. They also need the psychological and moral support of others who are and have been involved in the same situations.

Technical Support

Improving schools requires two sets of skills that few school leaders have had opportunity to acquire in their graduate work or have seen modeled in their own experience. The first of these is how to involve others in decision making. The other is how to use data in appropriate ways to guide the decision making. School districts need to provide their leaders with training in teamwork and group process skills and give them access to external facilitators when they need help and encouragement working with groups. Technical support in gathering and analyzing data and access to individuals with the expertise for statistical analysis is essential.

Networking

School districts need to coordinate collegial support for their leaders. Access to e-mail as a quick, informal way to communicate within the district and with more distant colleagues should be provided to every principal encountering new challenges of school change. Designating and coordinating mentor relationships is another form of networking that should occur through the district or professional associations. Just assigning a mentor is inadequate. Someone needs to be instrumental in setting times and places for them to communicate, helping them focus on needs and questions, and keeping the network active.

Active Listening

Recently, I spent time with the principal of three geographically remote schools. We talked about the uniqueness of her schools, and I asked her about her needs and ways the district could better assist her. She gave me a wistful look like that of a child staring through the window of a candy store, and I wondered whether I had created an expectation so great I'd surely fail to meet it. But with a sigh, all she said was, "What I need most is someone to talk to about all this, but I guess that's not the district's job. I guess it's a personal problem." She was both right and wrong. It is something she needs, and it is something the district should provide. Because her schools are very different from the others in the system, she hasn't been satisfied through her efforts to find a mentor among her peers. She has one now.

Purpose. In addition to having a specific person to share questions and concerns with, principals and other school leaders need opportunities to practice their own listening skills and interact with a wider range of colleagues. I first learned about a group process called Active Listening Trios from friends in the California School Leadership Academy. I have seen it adapted by several facilitators for use in a variety of other settings.

When to use. This group activity for active listening can be repeated every few months, focused on a common concern most relevant at that time. It can also be used after training in a new technique to identify and respond to concerns about implementation.

Whom to involve. One or more groups of three people who are willing to give each other 45 minutes of caring time are needed. The process can be used to increase communication and understanding among groups of teachers, within school leadership teams, in adult-student interactions, and even in families.

Materials needed. Active Listening Trios need a topic or concern as a focus and a timer to move the process along.

TIPS FOR FACILITATORS

Begin by reviewing the characteristics of active listening:

- Use of positive, open nonverbals
- Paraphrasing
- Asking probing questions
- Jotting down important points if the speaker consents
- Withholding advice until all the information is shared
- Hearing advice in full before reacting

Ask participants to form groups of three. There may be times when you structure the composition of the trios. For example, if a workshop setting includes people from several districts, I will encourage mixed groups as an opportunity to share ideas from other areas.

Within the trios, have one person designated as *A*, another as *B*, and the third as *C*. Provide a focus for their conversation, and overview the following steps so they have a grasp of the overall sequence:

Round 1

A shares and explains; *B* and *C* listen with no comment.

B and *C* ask clarifying questions only (no statements);
   A answers.

B and *C* offer advice and suggestions; *A* listens.

Round 2

B shares and explains; A and C listen with no comment.

A and C ask clarifying questions only (no statements);
    B answers.

A and C offer advice and suggestions; B listens.

Round 3

C shares and explains; A and B listen with no comment.

A and B ask clarifying questions only (no statements);
    C answers.

A and B offer advice and suggestions; C listens.

Establish a time limit for each step (4 minutes seems to work well) and select an unobtrusive signal for when to move on. Move a marker along an overhead transparency to provide a silent reminder of what to do next. Ask them to stay with the process even if they can't think of any more to say at that step. Remind them of the importance of "wait time" to let both speakers and listeners process at a deeper level.

After the exercise has been completed, encourage participants to share

- What they learned about their problem and about listening in general
- How it felt to be listened to without interruption for 4 minutes
- How it felt to be silent and not interrupt for 4 full minutes
- How they might use this exercise in other settings

FOR EXAMPLE

I conducted the Active Listening Trios exercise among a group of principals who responded to the prompt "My biggest concerns about shared decision making are . . ." The activity was well received, the participants discovered that they had many of the same concerns, they generated good strategies for dealing with them, and several made commitments to keep in touch and marked dates in their calendars to establish a set time for communication.

A few weeks later, I unexpectedly encountered one of the participants in a shopping mall. He said, "You're the one that did the listening thing, right?" I agreed and he went on to tell me how he and his wife had used the same process with a teenager in their home. He told me how embarrassed they were to discover that they had never spent even 4 whole minutes listening to his viewpoint on anything and how much mutual respect had been gained as all three of them got equal time to share their feelings.

In this chapter, we have explored partial answers to the question of "How will we sustain the focus and momentum?" Whether we create organizations that examine themselves and pursue continuous improvement depends, in large part, on how we treat those who carry the load on a daily basis. A most important aspect of leadership is nurturing the human resources of the organization through technical support, active listening, and caring responses.

8

Bonus Questions

S omewhere I heard that "no one likes change except a wet baby." The five critical questions examined in chapters 3-7 guide the process of school improvement. The "bonus" questions presented in this chapter address some of the effects of change on participants and observers.

Travelers on the road to school improvement know it is going to be a long trip with twists and turns and bumps along the way. But there are two things they should not have to experience. Their confidence should not be daunted or their past efforts demeaned. A danger with initiating change for the future is that it can feel to the "changees" like an accusation that everything they have done before is somehow wrong. The bonus questions "Did it make sense then?" and "Does it make sense now?" can be used to affirm the value of prior experience before moving into a new phase.

Traveling alone is no fun either. The need for networks and support was stressed in chapter 7. The bonus question "Who else?" encourages leaders to draw on the knowledge and interest of others and challenges us to accept our critical leadership role.

Did It Make Sense Then? Does It Make Sense Now?

A powerful phrase in the vocabulary of the 1980s was "paradigm shift." We all learned that a paradigm was an attitude or predisposition that governs our behavior, a perception held so strongly that it might not even be conscious, a filter through which we interpret

everything around us. Our paradigms determine what we will consider right and possible. Sometimes we get so locked into our paradigms that we suffer from "paradigm paralysis." The terminology
was so overused that it became discounted as another fad. In one
workshop I attended, a group member said, "I wouldn't give you two
cents for this stuff, let alone a pair o'dimes."

Even though the terminology became cliché, the concept is an
essential one. We have inherited and absorbed attitudes from our past
experience that are so strong we may not know they exist. We have
never questioned them, because we are unaware of them. We just
know that we get very uncomfortable with some new ideas that "just
don't feel right." Some groups have found it helpful to start "letting
go" by identifying things that have not changed about schools in the
past 50-100 years. Some of the items that appear on a typical list are
the following:

- 9 months of school
- Dismissing about 3:00
- Grade levels
- Carnegie units for high school graduation
- Self-contained elementary classrooms
- Departmentalized secondary schools
- A, B, C, D, and F grades
- Tracking college-bound and vocational

The next step is to revisit those structures of schooling with the
question "Did it make sense then?" The 9-month school year gets
linked to an agricultural economy, and we ask, "Did it make sense
then?" The answer is yes. So—good for us! Why did we dismiss
school about 3:00? The answer that eventually emerges is "because
factories ran a day shift that got out about 3:00." Did it make sense in
the industrial period? Yes? Well, good for us! What about Carnegie
units? Where did they come from? Many people don't know that
Carnegie pioneered the effort to identify some common standards as
prerequisites that would put students on a more even playing field
when they went on to a higher level of education. Did it make sense
in the days of rural schools to give them something to shoot for? Yes.
Then good for us as public educators! Conduct similar conversations
for the other items on the list and emphasize that those practices

didn't just emerge by happenstance. They were responses to the needs of society—the stakeholders—at that time. Encourage the participants to congratulate themselves and brag to each other about how customer oriented public education was even before that adjective was used.

When the celebration of pride dies down, pause and ask softly, "Does it make sense now?" Many groups act a little stunned by the question, but then they begin acknowledging that we do many things based on tradition, without thought about whether they still fit. They are also reassured when they realize that aspects of schooling we took for granted were once reforms themselves based on the needs of a changing society.

Use of these two questions will not lead to overnight restructuring and will not make the change process itself any easier. But they can help groups become more conscious of the origins of our traditions while reasserting pride in our past experience. From there, they can move on to preserving the things that still make sense and considering ways to change the things that don't. At the least, it's a far more positive experience than sitting in an auditorium for 3 hours while a zealot with a new cause castigates and humiliates us for being so outdated and so far behind every other decent country in the world.

Who Else . . . Should Be Included?

Organizations change as people within them change. That's one reason for the emphasis on participation and involvement in the study and planning phases of school improvement. Another reason is that organizational change is far too difficult and complex for one leader to be able to make it happen.

A veteran principal who was trying to make his own paradigm shift from benevolent dictator to a more shared approach discovered that he needed constant reminders to include others. In his wallet, on his daily calendar, and above the door inside his office, he placed the two words *Who Else?* As he analyzed a situation and prepared to "share decisions" by announcing what he had decided, those signs were his prompts to think about who else should have a voice. They would remind him to consider who else might have expertise to share, who else would be affected by the decision, and above all, whose cooperation was essential to making the decision work. By concentrating on these visual reminders, the experienced principal found himself receiving compliments from parents and staff on his "new leadership style."

Who Else . . . if Not Me?

Throughout the quality improvement literature, there are references to how 80% of the work in an organization is done by 20% of the people. Sometimes it seems like the improvement work in schools is done by only 2% of the people, and in an organization of 100 members, that 2% may feel like "me and my secretary." When we are discouraged and fatigued and tempted to ask "Why me?" we need to answer a question with a question: "Who else . . . if not me?" If I don't model perseverance, who else will? If I don't demonstrate continuous personal improvement, who else will care about ongoing professional and organizational improvement? If I don't reach out to meet our constituents halfway, who else will see the need to do so? The "Who else?" question can be a powerful tool in our own self-talk and motivation as leaders.

9

Using the Matrix

This book was born from a marriage of critical questions and group process techniques for teams to use to answer them. They have been organized into a matrix and offered as an aid for team leaders, facilitators, and consultants. My goal was that they be helpful in some of the following ways.

As a Quick Index to Your Toolbox

In chapter 1, I described an "out of the blue" request for advice on how to handle a group process challenge. You probably have those experiences too, and you are probably familiar with most or all of these group process techniques. They are already "in your toolbox."

A few days ago, I was asked to facilitate an activity but was cautioned "no flip charts and no circles." I was happy to agree, but curious. It turned out that a consultant on a long-term contract with the district had only one tool in his toolbox—get in a circle, no writing instruments or surfaces allowed, and reach consensus on everything including the color of marker he should use to write on the flip chart. Sometimes we get into a pattern of using one technique over and over and forget some of the others we have enjoyed using and found to be effective in other settings. One use of this matrix is to help us quickly scan the tools we have, so we can select one that will match the task before us.

When asked to facilitate an activity, get enough information to know what question the participants are trying to answer. Are they figuring out where they are now? Are they trying to set a goal? Are they deciding how to get there? Or are they simply struggling with some natural conflicts that are part of change and growth? Find their question on the left and move across the matrix to choose one of the group process techniques that addresses their need.

You have also developed skills that I didn't include in this book. The matrix has extra columns on the right where you can add headings for techniques you enjoy using. Think about the range of applications they have for answering the five critical questions. Place your own Xs in the cells of the matrix, and you have an even bigger toolbox than mine.

As a Tool for Planning Personal Skill Development

As you have read the book, you may have recognized every group process technique described. If so, skip this paragraph. If some of the activities were new to you, I'd suggest that you start like this. Get a highlighting pen and go across the top of the matrix. Highlight each technique you come to that you have used before and are confident you could facilitate with others. Go down each of those columns with the highlighter. Now you have a colored matrix to serve as a quick index to your own toolbox. You also have some "white spaces." These are the group process techniques you may wish to add to your toolbox. Consult the annotated bibliography and read more about them, find a workshop that includes them, or seek out a mentor who is willing to coach you as you practice them. This adds to your repertoire of skills and lets you color in more of the matrix as you develop new strategies.

As a Tool for Designing Team Training

Chapter 7 points out the importance of continued training to sustain the focus and momentum of change. One of the concepts mentioned is just-in-time training. This concept is particularly true for group process techniques. The prevalent pattern of sending a group of people to a conference on teamwork leaves many feeling as though they accomplished little real work, and transfer to their own setting is limited.

A more effective way to learn about teamwork is in the context of the immediate tasks that need to be accomplished. When you are asked to "give us some training in group techniques" or "teach us some strategies to use on our team," first get information on what the purpose of the team is and what tasks the participants are now trying to do. Use the matrix to identify techniques team members can use for the task at hand and design the content of their training to introduce techniques they can apply immediately. Provide time for them to plan how and when they will use the new technique and facilitate it with each other. One of the best ways to develop a sense of teamwork is to do real work as a team.

As a Tool for Coaching New Facilitators

The matrix can also be helpful as you work with cadres of internal trainers or as you coach new facilitators. Have them highlight the columns of the matrix under skills with which they feel comfortable. This provides a starting point. You can observe your facilitators using those techniques, to check their skill and provide feedback to help them refine their approaches. When you are also confident of their expertise in these areas, they can become coaches for others.

Also look at the white spaces they have not highlighted. Go across the matrix horizontally. If there is a whole section—one of the five critical questions—that is mostly white, start their new learning with a group process technique that will begin to fill in that gap.

Conclusion

There are ramblers and there are travelers. The ramblers will wind up where they will and probably won't remember how they got there. The travelers will probably reach their destination, especially if there are rest stops and information booths along the way. As leaders, change agents, and group facilitators, we staff the rest stops and information booths. If we provide adequate support and accurate guidance, the travelers are more likely to be interested in taking another trip, pursuing yet another destination of improvement.

May you find at least one of these techniques helpful,
at least one of these stories inspiring,
and as you nurture your organization's values,
may you find the strength to keep the faith!

Annotated Bibliography

Anderson, S. E., Rolheiser, C., & Bennett, B. (1995). Confronting the challenge of implementing cooperative learning. *Journal of Staff Development, 16,* 32-38.

This article describes use of the Stages of Concern Questionnaire to guide implementation of cooperative learning.

Bolman, L. G., & Deal, T. E. (1994). *Becoming a teacher leader: From isolation to collaboration.* Thousand Oaks, CA: Corwin.

This book is based on the authors' previous work describing organizations using the political, structural, human resource, and symbolic frameworks. The concepts are illustrated in story fashion, as two teachers discuss their changing roles.

Bonstingl, J. J. (1992). *Schools of quality: An introduction to total quality management in education.* Alexandria, VA: Association for Supervision and Curriculum Development.

Bonstingl's book provides a bridge between the business approach to quality management and the real world of schools. The appendixes are quick references to tools of quality and Deming's 14 Points.

Bullard, P., & Taylor, B. O. (1994). *Keepers of the dream: The triumph of effective schools.* Lake Forest, IL: Excelsior.

This book tells the stories of successful school reform efforts accomplished through effective schools programs across the United States. The voices of superintendents, principals, teachers, and community members are heard as they describe successful teamwork that changed their schools.

Fullan, M. G. (1993). *Change forces: Probing the depths of educational reform.* New York: Falmer.

This book represents Fullan's next stage of thinking after The Meaning of Educational Change *and* The New Meaning of Educational Change. *Where his previous work was rather technical and focused on structural issues, this book reveals a greater understanding of the complexity of change. Fullan places new emphasis on the importance of moral purpose and development of school culture as a learning organization.*

Fullan, M. G., & Stiegelbauer, S. M. (1991). *The new meaning of educational change.* New York: Teachers College Press.

This comprehensive look at school change combines research and practical application in a substantive but easily readable style. Discussion of the stages of initiation, implementation, and institutionalization or continuation appear in chapters 5 and 6. Part II is particularly helpful in school settings, describing the impact of change on teachers, principals, students, district administrators, parents, and communities.

Holcomb, E. L. (1991). *School-based instructional leadership: Staff development for teacher and school effectiveness.* Madison, WI: National Center for Effective Schools.

This multimedia training program includes participant's notebook, trainer's notebook, and Training of Trainers materials. It is designed in nine modules for use with cross-role teams of teachers, principals, other staff members, parents, and community members. A section on survey instruments and other resource materials is included. The program is now being distributed by Phi Delta Kappa. For information, contact Phil Harris, Center for Professional Development, PDK, 408 N. Union, Bloomington, IN 47402.

Holly, P. (1991). Action research: The missing link in the creation of schools as centers of inquiry. In A. Lieberman & L. Miller (Eds.), *Staff development for education in the '90s: New demands, new realities, new perspectives* (2nd ed., pp. 133-157). New York: Teachers College Press.

Holly provides a scholarly discussion of the historical development of action research and describes the stages of problem formulation, data collection, and data analysis.

Hord, S. M., Rutherford, W. L., Huling-Austin, L., & Hall, G. E. (1987). *Taking charge of change.* Alexandria, VA: Association for Supervision and Curriculum Development.

This book is an essential tool for diagnosing the concerns of individuals in change and helping the organization respond. It provides background information on development of the concerns-based adoption model and the Stages of Concern Questionnaire. Detailed explanations for use of the instrument and interpretation of profiles are included.

Johnson, D. W., & Johnson, F. P. (1994). *Joining together: Group theory and group skills.* Boston: Allyn & Bacon.

This book provides theoretical background on group dynamics, as well as practical advice for improving communication in groups, leading learning and discussion groups, and nurturing team development. The chapter on decision making is especially helpful with its clarification of consensus.

Katz, N. H., & Lawyer, J. W. (1994). *Resolving conflict successfully: Needed knowledge and skills.* Thousand Oaks, CA: Corwin.

The second of three volumes on conflict resolution for school administrators, this book provides helpful information on building rapport, reflective listening, and problem solving.

Lezotte, L., & Jacoby, B. (1990). *A guide to the school improvement process based on effective schools research.* Okemos, MI: Effective Schools Products.

This handbook outlines the school improvement process and provides sample forms, timelines, and practical suggestions for implementation.

Loucks-Horsley, S., & Stiegelbauer, S. M. (1991). Using knowledge of change to guide staff development. In A. Lieberman & L. Miller (Eds.), *Staff development for education in the '90s: New demands, new realities, new perspectives* (2nd ed., pp. 15-36). New York: Teachers College Press.

This chapter provides an overview of the concerns-based adoption model and a description of how to use the Stages of Concern Questionnaire to plan staff development programs.

McManus, A. (1992). *The memory jogger for education: A pocket guide of tools for continuous improvement in schools.* Methuen, MA: GOAL/QPC.

This booklet was adapted from a similar guide for business that was compiled and edited by Michael Brassard. It provides diagrams and brief instructions for use of statistical tools such as histograms, run charts, and control charts.

Scholtes, P. R. (1988). *The team handbook: How to use teams to improve quality.* Madison, WI: Joiner.

This handbook reviews the basics of quality improvement and describes the use of statistical tools for quality improvement. It also includes chapters on forming a project team, guidelines for productive meetings, building improvement plans, and team dynamics. It is very helpful for readers who can create their own bridges between the business context and schools.

Taylor, B. O., & Bullard, P. (1995). *The revolution revisited: Effective schools and systemic reform.* Bloomington, IN: Phi Delta Kappa.

This small booklet is filled with a collection of reports that update the development of the effective schools process in schools nationwide. The comprehensive systemic process is described in detail by the authors and practitioners whose schools have profited from its implementation.

Wood, F. H. (1989). Organizing and managing school-based staff development. In S. D. Caldwell (Ed.), *Staff development: A handbook of effective practices* (pp. 26-43). Oxford, OH: National Staff Development Council.

In this chapter, Wood describes the stages of readiness, planning, training, implementation, and maintenance that have become known as the RPTIM model. A section on districtwide staff development for school-based improvement is helpful for central office administrators.

Index

Action planning:
    example of, for mentor
        program, 73-77
    involvement in, 72
    materials needed for, 72
    purpose of, 71, 79
    tips for use of, 72-73
    when to use, 4-6, 71-72
Action research:
    example of, 102
    involvement in, 100
    materials needed for, 100-101
    purpose of, 99-100
    tips for use of, 101-102, 121
    when to use, 4-6, 100
Active listening:
    example of, 110-111
    involvement in, 109
    materials needed for, 109
    purpose of, 108
    tips for use of, 109-110
    when to use, 4-6, 109
Advocacy statement, 43
Affinity process:
    example of, 45
    involvement in, 42
    materials needed for, 42
    purpose of, 41

    tips for use of, 42-44
    when to use, 4-6, 42
Aggregate data, 15. *See also*
    Disaggregation
Anderson, S.E., 83, 120
Association for Supervision and
    Curriculum Development
    (ASCD), 105, 120, 122

Bennett, B., 83, 120
Brainstorming:
    examples of, 47, 49, 55-56, 69
    involvement in, 46
    materials needed for, 46
    purpose of, 46
    tips for use of, 46-47
    when to use, 4-6, 46

California School Leadership
    Academy (CSLA), 108
Cause-and-effect diagram
    (fishbone):
    example of, for absenteeism,
        62-65
    involvement in, 60-61
    materials needed for, 61

purpose of, 60
tips for use of, 61-62
when to use, 4-6, 60
Character education, 89-90
Citizenship, 81
Coaching, 87-88, 103, 118
Color coding:
    examples of, 25, 55
    involvement in, 54
    materials needed for, 54
    purpose of, 54
    tips for use of, 55
    when to use, 4-6, 54
Community, 12
Computer:
    use of graphic software, 16,
        20, 22, 29, 36
    use of laptop, 16, 27, 50, 68, 72
Concerns-Based Adoption
    Model (CBAM), 81-82,
    122-123. *See also* Stages of
    Concern Questionnaire
Conflict management:
    Cause-and-effect diagram
        for, 60
    Go for the Green for, 96-98
    Quick-Writes for, 90-92
    TalkWalks for, 93-95
    Think, Pair, Share for, 32-35
    Venn diagrams for, 88-90
Continuous improvement, 111,
    115. *See also* Action
    Research, School
    Improvement Process
Cooperative learning, 101-102,
    105, 120

Data. *See* Disaggregation,
    Quartiles, Student
    achievement data,
    Student attendance data,
    Socioeconomic status

Deal, T.E., 107, 120
Decision matrix:
    examples of, 69-71
    involvement in, 68
    materials needed for, 68
    purpose of, 60, 68
    tips for use of, 68-69
    when to use, 4-6, 68
Disaggregation:
    in histogram, 19
    in run chart, 23
    by socioeconomic status, 17
District office role, 72, 95, 101,
    104, 107, 121, 123

Edmonds, R., 63, 106
Effective schools:
    factors of, in surveys, 24, 28
    reform efforts based on,
        120-123
    research base of, 2, 9, 63, 95,
        106
Elmore, R., 10

Fishbone. *See* Cause-and-effect
    diagram
Flowcharting:
    examples of, 36-39
    involvement in, 36
    materials needed for, 36
    purpose of, 35
    tips for use of, 36
    when to use, 4-6, 35
Focus groups:
    example of, 28
    involvement in, 26-27
    materials needed for, 27
    purpose of, 26
    tips for use of, 27
    when to use, 4-6, 26

Force field analysis:
    example of, 66-67
    involvement in, 65-66
    materials needed for, 66
    purpose of, 60, 65
    tips for use of, 66
    when to use, 4-6, 65
Fullan, M.G., 9-11, 107, 121

Garmston, R., 42, 96
Go for the Green:
    example of, 97-98
    involvement in, 96
    materials needed for, 96
    purpose of, 96
    tips for use of, 96-97
    when to use, 4-6, 96
Group process techniques, 1, 3,
        4-6, 107, 116-118

Histogram:
    examples of, 17-19
    involvement in, 16
    materials needed for, 16
    purpose of, 15-16
    tips for use of, 16-17
    when to use, 4-6, 16
Homeless students, 31-32
Horizontal axis:
    on pareto chart, 29
    on run chart, 22
Huberman, M., 10-11
Hunter, M., 80

Implementation, 4-6, 10-11, 13,
        59, 79, 86
Initiation, 4-6, 10-12, 59
Institutionalization, 4-6, 10-11,
        13, 79, 86
Instructional time, 21

Jacoby, B., 9, 122
Joplin plan, 69-70
Just-in-time training, 87, 117

Leadership teams, 12, 32
    role of, in action research, 100
    role of, in force field analysis,
        65
    role of, in mission, 40, 44, 47,
        84-85
    training of, 56-58, 94-95
Learning styles, 71, 101, 104
Lezotte, L.W., 9, 40, 63, 106, 122
Lifelong learner, 47-48, 73

Maintenance, 4-6, 10, 13, 79, 86
Matrix of group process
        techniques, 4-6, 10, 116-118
Mentors:
    for chronic absentees, 62-65,
        73-77
    for facilitators, 117
    for principals, 108
Merit pay, 37
Metaphors:
    of change as corkscrew, 99
    of change as journey, 14, 40,
        42, 59, 66-67, 78-79, 86-87,
        112, 118-119
    to diagnose culture, 33, 37, 39
    of involvement, 45
    of sustained focus, 86
Miles, M., 10-11
Mission:
    in decision matrix, 69
    examples of, 45
    fulfilling, in school culture,
        44, 79, 84-85, 103
    importance of, 40-41
    observable indicators of, 41,
        47-48, 73, 79-80

process for developing, 41-44
Multiage classrooms, 70-72
Multiple intelligences, 71

Networking, 108, 112
Nominal group process:
    examples of, 51-54
    involvement in, 48
    materials needed for, 48
    purpose of, 48
    tips for use of, 49
    when to use, 4-6, 48

Observable indicators, 13, 41,
    47-48, 73, 79-81
Organized abandonment, 106

Paradigms, 87, 112-114
Parent involvement, 26, 35, 69,
    72, 80. *See also*
    Community, Stakeholders
Pareto charts:
    examples of 29-32
    involvement in, 29
    materials needed for, 29
    purpose of, 29
    tips for use of, 29
    when to use, 4-6, 29
Phonics, 69-70
Pie charts:
    example of, 21
    involvement in, 20
    materials needed for, 20
    purpose of, 20
    tips for use of, 20
    when to use, 4-6, 20-21
Plan-Do-Check-Act cycle, 4-6,
    11-13, 40, 59, 79, 86
Planning, 4-6, 10, 12, 40, 59
Portable classrooms, 70-71

Priorities:
    color coding to set, 54-55
    need for, 41, 48
    nominal group process to set,
        48-52
    weighted voting to set, 55-58

Quartiles, 17
Quick-Writes:
    example of, 91-92
    involvement in, 91
    materials needed for, 91
    purpose of, 90
    tips for use of, 91
    when to use, 4-6, 90-91

Readiness, 4-6, 10-12
Reading achievement, 22-23,
    69-70
Reflective study groups:
    examples of, 105-106
    involvement in, 104
    materials needed for, 104
    purpose of, 103-104
    tips for use of, 104-105
    when to use, 4-6, 104
Resistance, 9, 24, 36, 61-65, 87,
    105, 107
Ripken, Cal, Jr., 86
Robbins, Pam, 93
Rolheiser, Carol, 83, 120
RPTIM model, 4-6, 10-12, 40, 59,
    79, 86, 123
Run charts:
    example of, 22-23
    involvement in, 22
    materials needed for, 22
    purpose of, 21
    tips for use of, 22
    when to use, 4-6, 22

School culture, 4, 6, 11, 15, 84,
    86-87
  celebrating, 106-107
  tools to diagnose, 33, 35-39,
    93, 104
School improvement process, 9,
    24, 62, 99, 112, 114-115,
    122-123
Sergiovanni, T.J., 107
Side conversations in meetings,
    97-98
Site-based management, 2,
    35-37, 91-92
Socioeconomic status (SES):
  for disaggregating data, 17,
    19, 22
  related to attendance, 63-65
  related to reading
    achievement, 23
Stages of Concern
    Questionnaire (SoCQ):
  example of, 83
  involvement in, 82
  materials needed for, 82
  as one-legged interview, 83-84
  purpose of, 82
  tips for use of, 83, 120,
    122-123
  when to use, 4-6, 82
  for workshop feedback, 84
Stakeholders:
  definition of, 11-12, 23
  involvement of, 23, 25, 42-44,
    54, 60, 91-92, 100, 114
  minority, 25-26
  representativeness of, 23-24,
    25, 27
Stratified sampling, 24-25
Student achievement, 14-23,
    52-54, 79-80
Student attendance, 62-65, 73-77

Student discipline, 15, 20, 29-31,
    85
Student recognition, 28
Success for All, 69-70
Surveys:
  costs of, 24
  design of, 23, 25
  example of, 25-26
  formal, 23, 24, 28
  informal, 23, 24
  involvement in, 24
  materials needed for, 24-25
  purpose of, 23
  rate of return in, 24
  stratified sampling in, 24-25
  tips for use of, 25, 121
  when to use, 4-6, 24

TalkWalks:
  example of, 94-95
  involvement in, 93
  materials needed for, 93
  purpose of, 93
  tips for use of, 94
  when to use, 4-6, 93
Tape recorder, 27
Team teaching, 70-71
Teamwork training, 2, 107, 118,
    121
Thematic analysis, 26
Think, Pair, Share:
  examples of, 33-35
  involvement in, 32-33
  materials needed for, 33
  purpose of, 32
  tips for use of, 33
  when to use, 4-6, 32
Three Is model, 4-6, 11-13, 59, 79,
    86, 121
Total quality management, 11,
    31, 41, 61, 87, 115, 120, 123

Training:
    in RPTIM model, 4-6, 10, 59
    in *Three Is* model, 4-6, 11-12
    to sustain effort, 87-88
TYNT-NYNT, 10

University partnerships, 99-101

Venn diagrams:
    example of 89-90
    involvement in, 89
    materials needed for, 89
    purpose of, 88
    tips for use of, 89
    when to use, 4-6, 89

Vertical axis:
    on pareto chart, 29
    on run chart, 22

Wait time, 27, 47, 69, 110
Weighted voting:
    example of, 56-58
    involvement in, 56
    materials needed for, 56
    purpose of, 56
    tips for use of, 56
    when to use, 4-6, 56
Whole language, 69-70
Wood, F.H., 10, 123

Year-round school, 66-67

CORWIN
PRESS

The Corwin Press logo—a raven striding across an open book—represents the happy union of courage and learning. We are a professional-level publisher of books and journals for K–12 educators, and we are committed to creating and providing resources that embody these qualities. Corwin's motto is "Success for All Learners."